ॐ

श्रीमदष्टावक्र गीता

śrīmad-aṣṭāvakra-gītā

⌘

ashtavakra gita

a fiery octave in ascension

⌘⌘

Belongs to ____________________

⌘⌘⌘

Sanskrit Text with English Translation

(Convenient 4"x6" Pocket-Sized Edition)

Published by: only **RAMA** only
(an Imprint of e1i1 Corporation)

Title: Ashtavakra Gita, A Fiery Octave in Ascension
Sub-Title: Sanskrit Text with English Translation
(Convenient 4"x6" Pocket-Sized Edition)

Original Sanskrit Text: Ashtāvakra (Prehistoric Sage)
Author-Translator: Vidya Wati

Identifiers
ISBN: 978-1-945739-48-4 (Paperback)

—o—

This Book is also available in following formats:

(1) Ashtāvakra Gītā, a Fiery Octave in Ascension
ISBN: **978-1-945739-46-0** (Paperback)
ISBN: **978-1-945739-47-7** (Hardcover)
(Regular book size: 6.14"x9.21")

(2) Ashtāvakra Gītā, the Fiery Octave
My Self: the Ātmā Journal -- A Daily Journey of Self Discovery
ISBN: **978-1-945739-42-2** (Paperback)
(A Journal Book sized 7.5"x9.25" having 365 pages with space for taking notes and journaling your daily thoughts alongside the verses.)

—⌘—

श्रीमदष्टावक्र गीता - śrīmadaṣṭāvakra gītā

११ • प्रथमोऽध्यायः Canto I – Instructions on Self-Realization • 11

१९ • द्वितीयोऽध्यायः Canto II – Reveling as the Ātmā • 19

२९ • तृतीयोऽध्यायः Canto III – Veracity of Self-Realization • 29

३५ • चतुर्थोऽध्यायः Canto IV – Glory of Self-Realization • 35

३८ • पञ्चमोऽध्यायः Canto V – Dissolution • 38

४० • षष्ठोऽध्यायः Canto VI – Supreme Truth • 40

४२ • सप्तमोऽध्यायः Canto VII – Describing Self-Realization • 42

४४ • अष्टमोऽध्यायः Canto VIII – Bondage and Liberation • 44

४६ • नवमोऽध्यायः Canto IX – Aloofness • 46

५० • दशमोऽध्यायः Canto X – Equanimity • 50

५४ • एकादशोऽध्यायः Canto XI – Wisdom • 54

५८ • द्वादशोऽध्यायः Canto XII – Onlyness • 58

६२ • त्रयोदशोऽध्यायः Canto XIII – Felicity • 62

६५ • चतुर्दशोऽध्यायः Canto XIV – Tranquility • 65

६७ • पञ्चदशोऽध्यायः Canto XV – Essence of Self-Knowledge • 67

७६ • षोडशोऽध्यायः Canto XVI – Special Instruction • 76

८१ • सप्तदशोऽध्यायः Canto XVII – The Self-Realized Sage • 81

८९ • अष्टादशोऽध्यायः Canto XVIII – Serenity • 89

१२५ • एकोनविंशतिकोऽध्यायः Canto XIX – Reposing as the Ātmā • 125

१२८ • विंशतिकोऽध्यायः Canto XX – Liberation-in-Life • 128

— ॐ —

A Brief Note

Ashtāvakra Gītā, a Vedāntic scripture from ancient India, is a dialogue between a disciple (King Janaka) and a Master (Muni Ashtāvakra). Janaka, the King of Mithīlā, is also well-known as the father of Shri-Sītā, the divine consort of Lord Shri-Rāma whose glories are sung in the Rāmāyana. Ashtāvakra was a great ascetic and a realized soul who had attained liberation while alive. As was customary in ancient India he would roam the land to light the lamp of wisdom in the minds of others and show people the path to happiness and this conversation takes place during one such sojourn when he happens to meet King Janaka.

Ashtāvakra literally means Eight-Curved and as the legend goes Ashtāvakra's body was bent in eight places—though some would find it difficult to conceive of a body so extremely deformed. Who knows what Ashtāvakra really looked like—it's immaterial. The only thing we have to go by is the text of Ashtāvakra Gītā (Ashtāvakra's Song) which has come down to us across several millenniums and we like to think of it as a song of eight-notes in a Fiery Ascent. Ashtāvakra Gītā is a Fiery Octave in Ascension transporting the Jīvas into the realm of Brahama over the centuries. Our repeated salutations to the exalted sage Ashtāvakra, who surely must have been a most beautiful soul.

In this scripture Ashtāvakra expounds on Jnāna-Yoga—gaining emancipation following the path of

Self-Knowledge. Traversing the winding course of a tortuous life, a person may finally come to the conclusion that happiness cannot be found in the things of the world. If fortunate enough he will then pursue some path of Vedic Dharma to escape misery and gain happiness; Jnāna is one such path and following that path the aspirant will realize the true nature of the Self and attain to peace—finally becoming liberated from the endless sufferings of the world. Scriptures like this guide us on the path to Jnāna—which lands us directly at the very portal of Nirvana.

Be warned though: having fully come by wisdom (Jnāna)—having realized that the Self and the Supreme-Self are one, that all this is just One-Consciousness sporting and that there is no 'other' here—the journey of the soul forthwith comes to an end. When the sage directly realizes that there simply is nothing else except the One-Singularity, then all actions and impulses become ended; there is no impetus for one to move any further. This is a rare high state—hard to attain—and having reached there the Yogi does not abide in the body for long—with the body dropping away from him soon thereafter.

If everyone were to become fully realized in the Oneness of Brahama, then this sport of life will continue no further. According to the Vedas the world was created by the Supreme-Being to sport, to delight in the universe—because at one time He was all alone and therefore He decided to become many. So then, even after having come by perfect Jnāna, some Yogis choose not to enter the final Nirvana in

Brahama—but instead they flit in and out of the highest state. They reach the state of freedom but then descend to sport in the world—abiding as Liberated-in-Life—choosing to remain bound traversing the paths of Bhakti/Karma while also fully dwelling in Jnāna of course.

Over the millenniums in India most exalted sages have regarded Jnāna not to be an end in itself; they rather spurn Moksha and choose Bhakti—as you will discover when you read the writings of Goswami Tulsidasa, a saint from 16th century India; or some like King Janaka of this book, born millenniums ago, choose the path of Karma-Yoga—continuing to perform duties unattached even after having attained Realization; and there are innumerous other such examples in Vedic literature.

The path of Karma-Bhakti-Jnāna is an all rounded approach to spiritual life which has been beautifully laid out in the astounding scripture Bhagavada-Gītā. Likewise Tulsidas' Rāmāyana shows us a similar path of Bhakti-Karma-Jnāna—with special emphasis on Bhakti as the principal means to be pursued in life. Both are excellent scriptures and we recommend that the readers study these texts diligently if they wish to gain an all-rounded understanding of Vedic-Dharma.

No doubt Vedāntic texts like this are also necessary to help us in our spiritual endeavors. Bhakti and Karma would, by themselves, become insufferable if bereft of Jnāna (—because without the eyes of Jnāna, without the accompanying wisdom, Karma and Bhakti may lead aspirants down blind pitfalls). But pure Jnāna by itself leads straight to Moksha—where the body falls away and the soul forever merges in the Absolute.

Which path to pursue in life—whether that of pure Jnāna-Vairāgya-Jnāna as espoused in Vedantic scriptures like this one, or the paths of Bhakti-Karma-Jnāna as laid out in the Tulsi-Rāmāyana, or the paths of Karma-Bhakti-Jnāna as laid out in the Bhagavada-Gītā depends on one's choosing and destiny in life—surely one's own heart knows.

To reiterate, this is an important scripture but study of arrant Vedāntic thoughts like this must be attended with the study of Bhagavada-Gītā/Tulsi-Rāmāyana—and vice-versa. Most readers are already familiar with those and this cautionary note may not apply to them, but for those are untutored in Hindu Dharma and who may have simply stumbled on this book, we feel compelled to explicitly sound this note of caution. Reason being that you will find certain verses in Vedānta which seemingly appear to give blanket permission to give up all karmas, or then again do whatever pleases one's heart—all in the name of Vedānta—holding to the blank check of "I am Brahama, the Supreme Absolute, the Lord-God", and so anything goes. But if one is not careful and chooses to become "selective" in Vedāntic do's and don'ts, it will lead to one's downfall. Not only certain charlatans have been fooling the masses calling themselves God and shamelessly doing ritual worships like Shiva-Abhisheka upon their own person in the name of "Shivoham—I am Shiva", but it is quite possible that a genuine aspirant might himself go astray on this path inadvertently, without even realizing it or admitting it to himself, especially in this day and age of the Kali-Yuga. Human mind is easily corrupted and may well go astray and we need the Bhagavada-Gītā/Tulsi-Rāmāyana to keep us firmly rooted in Vedic Dharma.

Lest one fall in the path of "Aham-Brahama-Āsmi" and come to grief, let us first begin by having a balanced approach—studying Bhakti, Karma, Jnāna, Vairāgya all together. Of course this is no advice but just a personal opinion; most aspirants will walk the path their own heart bids they follow.

Distorted and full of inaccuracies, we feel much ashamed to call this work a translation—rather it is just a bunch of English words thrown by us at the original Sanskrit underframe in the hope that some of it will stick and take on a shape to mimic the original—which seminal text itself is sublime and inimitable, and inimical to translation. The meanings of verses given here is just a feeble attempt to present the essence—with many extraneous words of our own added—out of foolishness and bravado—and we sincerely seek forgiveness of the discriminating readers and the hallowed memory of the exalted sage Ashtāvakra for committing this sacrilege: pray take pity!

Wishing you the very best in your spiritual journey!!

— ॐ —

ॐ

श्रीअष्टावक्रविरचितं

śrīaṣṭāvakraviracitaṁ

॥ श्रीमदष्टावक्र गीता ॥

śrīmadaṣṭāvakra gītā

—::—

the

śrīmad-aṣṭāvakra-gītā

composed by

śrī-ashtāvakra

ॐ

ॐ पूर्णमदः पूर्णमिदँ पूर्णात् पूर्णमुदच्यते ।

om pūrṇamadaḥ pūrṇamidaṁ pūrṇāt pūrṇamudacyate ,

पूर्णस्य पूर्णमादाय पूर्णमेवावशिष्यते ।

pūrṇasya pūrṇamādāya pūrṇamevāvaśiṣyate ,

ॐ शान्तिः शान्तिः शान्तिः ॥

om śāntiḥ śāntiḥ śāntiḥ .

Om: That One (the Unmanifest Brahama)—is infinite, complete, entire; this (the manifest universe) is entire; And from That One fullness of Brahama has emerged this here entireness of creation; And even when this here worldly entirety is taken out of that One Entire, Brahama still abides complete in all Its entireness!

Om, peace, peace, peace !

Let there be tranquility all around !!

:: Canto – I ::
- Instructions on Self-Realization -

जनक उवाच
janaka uvāca:

कथं ज्ञानमवाप्नोति कथं मुक्तिर्भविष्यति ।
katham jñānamavāpnoti katham muktirbhaviṣyati ,
वैराग्यं च कथं प्राप्तमेतद् ब्रूहि मम प्रभो ॥ १-१ ॥
vairāgyaṁ ca kathaṁ prāptametad brūhi mama prabho (1-1)

Janaka said:
Please O Master,
How can wisdom be gained?
How can liberation be attained?
And how is dispassion to be acquired?
Please explicate at length.

[Please note that King Janaka, although a disciple, is already well-tutored and adept in the path of Vedānta. He just wishes to hear of the same once again from Ashtāvakra—just for the joy of listening to his favorite theme from a great Master.]

अष्टावक्र उवाच
aṣṭāvakra uvāca:

मुक्तिमिच्छसि चेत्तात विषयान् विषवत्त्यज ।
muktimicchasi cettāta viṣayān viṣavattyaja ,
क्षमार्जवदयातोषसत्यं पीयूषवद् भज ॥ १-२ ॥
kṣamārjavadayātoṣasatyaṁ pīyūṣavad bhaja (1-2)

Ashtāvakra said:
My child,
if you aspire for liberation
then at the very outset
shun the objects of the senses like poison itself;
and then acquire the nectars of
Tolerance,
Ārjava (simplicity, innocence, naturalness),
Compassion, Contentment and Truthfulness.

न पृथ्वी न जलं नाग्निर्न वायुर्द्यौर्न वा भवान् ।
na pṛthvī na jalaṁ nāgnirna vāyurdyaurna vā bhavān ,
एषां साक्षिणमात्मानं चिद्रूपं विद्धि मुक्तये ॥ १-३ ॥
eṣāṁ sākṣiṇamātmānaṁ cidrūpaṁ viddhi muktaye (1-3)

Realize that you are not the body made up of the elements;
you are not comprised of earth, water, fire, air, aether.
Know yourself to be purely a Consciousness
—the Self, in and as Itself—
a mere Witness to all this play;
and that is the way to attain emancipation.

यदि देहं पृथक् कृत्य चिति विश्राम्य तिष्ठसि ।
yadi dehaṁ pṛthak kṛtya citi viśrāmya tiṣṭhasi ,
अधुनैव सुखी शान्तो बन्धमुक्तो भविष्यसि ॥ १-४ ॥
adhunaiva sukhī śānto bandhamukto bhaviṣyasi (1-4)

When you have discerned the Self as abiding distinct from all this visible
—discovered your Self to be just a consciousness reclining within a sheath called the body—
you shall forthwith stand freed of bondages and attain to the state of peace and happiness
—even here, even now.

न त्वं विप्रादिको वर्णो नाश्रमी नाक्षगोचरः ।
na tvaṁ viprādiko varṇo nāśramī nākṣagocaraḥ ,
असङ्गोऽसि निराकारो विश्वसाक्षी सुखी भव ॥ १-५ ॥
asaṅgo'si nirākāro viśvasākṣī sukhī bhava (1-5)

You do not belong to *Brahmin* etc., castes
or any of the *Āshramas*—the four orders of life;
you are not anything that can be perceived by the sense-organs.
At your very essence,
you are bodyless, formless, unattached—
merely a Witness to this play being enacted here.
When you realize this directly,
you shall attain happiness.

धर्माधर्मौ सुखं दुःखं मानसानि न ते विभो ।
dharmādharmau sukhaṁ duḥkhaṁ mānasāni na te vibho ,
न कर्तासि न भोक्तासि मुक्त एवासि सर्वदा ॥ १-६ ॥
na kartāsi na bhoktāsi mukta evāsi sarvadā (1-6)

Virtue and vice, pleasure and pain,
—these are just of the mind alone,
and these are of no concern to thee,
O thou all-pervading pristine consciousness!
Thou art neither the doer
nor the partaker of anything here.
Thou art just the Ātmā:
ever free,
beyond any of this play.

एको द्रष्टासि सर्वस्य मुक्तप्रायोऽसि सर्वदा ।
eko draṣṭāsi sarvasya muktaprāyo'si sarvadā ,
अयमेव हि ते बन्धो द्रष्टारं पश्यसीतरम् ॥ १-७ ॥
ayameva hi te bandho draṣṭāraṁ paśyasītaram (1-7)

Of this drama of Rāma,
you are merely a Witness
—ever free,
bound to nothing here.
Alas, this alone is your bondage:
that you see yourself not as the Seer aloof
but as someone other than that—
a captive participant ...hapless.

अहं कर्तेत्यहंमानमहाकृष्णाहिदंशितः ।
ahaṁ kartetyahaṁmānamahākṛṣṇāhidaṁśitaḥ ,
नाहं कर्तेति विश्वासामृतं पीत्वा सुखी भव ॥ १-८ ॥
nāhaṁ karteti viśvāsāmṛtaṁ pītvā sukhī bhava (1-8)

May thou
—who have been bitten by the deadly serpent of egoism,
who persist delirious in its venom,
hallucinating, "I am the doer"—
drink of the antidote of faith

—partake of the curative reality—
which avers: "I am Not the doer";
and replete with that nectar,
may thou abide ever glad.

एको विशुद्धबोधोऽहमिति निश्चयवह्निना ।
eko viśuddhabodho'hamiti niścayavahninā ,
प्रज्वाल्याज्ञानगहनं वीतशोकः सुखी भव ॥१-९॥
prajvālyājñānagahanaṁ vītaśokaḥ sukhī bhava (1-9)

Burn down this wilderness of Ignorance in the
Fiery Knowledge-of-the-Self,
the essence of which Truth is the firm conviction that proclaims,
"I am the One Reality,
the all-pervading pristine Consciousness";
and thus freed of pain grief sorrows,
may thou abide in supreme happiness.

यत्र विश्वमिदं भाति कल्पितं रज्जुसर्पवत् ।
yatra viśvamidaṁ bhāti kalpitaṁ rajjusarpavat ,
आनन्दपरमानन्दः स बोधस्त्वं सुखं भव ॥१-१०॥
ānandaparamānandaḥ sa bodhastvaṁ sukhaṁ bhava (1-10)

That Supreme-One,
upon whom this universe appears superimposed,
—just like a snake is imagined upon a rope in darkness—
That One-Consciousness,
of the innate nature of Bliss
—Supreme-Bliss—
is who you really are!
Giving up ignorance and realizing That directly,
may you thereby abide in happiness.

मुक्ताभिमानी मुक्तो हि बद्धो बद्धाभिमान्यपि ।
muktābhimānī mukto hi baddho baddhābhimānyapi ,
किंवदन्तीह सत्येयं या मतिः सा गतिर्भवेत् ॥१-११॥
kiṁvadantīha satyeyaṁ yā matiḥ sā gatirbhavet (1-11)

He who considers himself free, free indeed he is;
and he who believes himself to be bound,

bound he remains.
"As one thinks, so one becomes",
—is a popular worldly phrase,
and so true.

आत्मा साक्षी विभुः पूर्ण एको मुक्तश्चिदक्रियः ।
ātmā sākṣī vibhuḥ pūrṇa eko muktaścidakriyaḥ ,
असङ्गो निःस्पृहः शान्तो भ्रमात्संसारवानिव ॥ १-१२ ॥
asaṅgo niḥspṛhaḥ śānto bhramātsaṁsāravāniva (1-12)

Not the body or the mind
but you are just only the Ātmā
—all-pervading, self-existent, self-sufficient, perfect and complete;
bereft of action and merely a Witness
to all this that you see.
Aye, you are only the Ātmā
—the One-Consciousness,
unattached, desireless,
ever free and ever in peace,
completely unlike the body
or anything from the manifest world
—although by dint of your delusions
the Self may appear to be just the mind and body only.

कूटस्थं बोधमद्वैतमात्मानं परिभावय ।
kūṭasthaṁ bodhamadvaitamātmānaṁ paribhāvaya ,
आभासोऽहं भ्रमं मुक्त्वा भावं बाह्यमथान्तरम् ॥ १-१३ ॥
ābhāso'haṁ bhramaṁ muktvā bhāvaṁ bāhyamathāntaram (1-13)

Giving up the mistaken identification with the body
—the external crust—
and rid also of identifying yourself
as being the ego and mind
—the superimposed delusions which are but reflections of the Ātmā—
meditate on yourself as being none of those but purely the Ātmā pure: Immutable Consciousness,
the One without a second.

देहाभिमानपाशेन चिरं बद्धोऽसि पुत्रक ।
dehābhimānapāśena ciraṁ baddho'si putraka ,
बोधोऽहं ज्ञानखड्गेन तन्निकृत्य सुखी भव ॥ १-१४ ॥
bodho'haṁ jñānakhaḍgena tannikṛtya sukhī bhava (1-14)

For long now you have been ensnared in the trap of,
"considering the Self to be identical to the body".
With the sharp sword of knowledge
break this bondage now,
averring:
"I am a pure consciousness and nothing else"
... and this way abide ever glad, my son.

निःसङ्गो निष्क्रियोऽसि त्वं स्वप्रकाशो निरञ्जनः ।
niḥsaṅgo niṣkriyo'si tvaṁ svaprakāśo nirañjanaḥ ,
अयमेव हि ते बन्धः समाधिमनुतिष्ठति ॥ १-१५ ॥
ayameva hi te bandhaḥ samādhimanutiṣṭhati (1-15)

In truth you already are unfettered and free
—being the Ātmā which is always unattached, actionless, self-effulgent and without any blemishes.
And this indeed is your bondage:
that you think you are the mind,
and then resort desperately to making that mind still,
in deep meditations.

त्वया व्याप्तमिदं विश्वं त्वयि प्रोतं यथार्थतः ।
tvayā vyāptamidaṁ viśvaṁ tvayi protaṁ yathārthataḥ ,
शुद्धबुद्धस्वरूपस्त्वं मा गमः क्षुद्रचित्तताम् ॥ १-१६ ॥
śuddhabuddhasvarūpastvaṁ mā gamaḥ kṣudracittatām (1-16)

This entire universe is strung out in You!
You are verily the Supreme,
the Singularity of the Absolute,
the One-Pristine-Consciousness
pervading throughout the entirety of existence!!
O, stop being petty minded and timid
—and realize your own Infinite Glory already!!!

निरपेक्षो निर्विकारो निर्भरः शीतलाशयः ।
nirapekṣo nirvikāro nirbharaḥ śītalāśayaḥ ,
अगाधबुद्धिरक्षुब्धो भव चिन्मात्रवासनः ॥१-१७॥
agādhabuddhirakṣubdho bhava cinmātravāsanaḥ (1-17)

You are a pristine consciousness
—self-sufficient,
free of modifications, unaffected,
imperturbable, tranquil,
nameless, formless, unfathomable—
which shines as pure Intelligence.
So always abide in just your true essence—
holding to nothing but your real Self:
the Ātmā
—getting rid of all the taints you have superimposed and accumulated upon that Self.

साकारमनृतं विद्धि निराकारं तु निश्चलम् ।
sākāramanṛtaṁ viddhi nirākāraṁ tu niścalam ,
एतत्तत्त्वोपदेशेन न पुनर्भवसम्भवः ॥१-१८॥
etattattvopadeśena na punarbhavasambhavaḥ (1-18)

"That which has a form
is necessarily non-lasting, non-Real
—it must meet its end;
and it is only the Unmanifest Reality
which abides everlastingly."
Initiated into this High Truth
—and having realized it directly—
you shall escape falling back
into the vicious birth-death cycle once again.

यथैवादर्शमध्यस्थे रूपेऽन्तः परितस्तु सः ।
yathaivādarśamadhyasthe rūpe'ntaḥ paritastu saḥ ,
तथैवाऽस्मिन् शरीरेऽन्तः परितः परमेश्वरः ॥१-१९॥
tathaivā'smin śarīre'ntaḥ paritaḥ parameśvaraḥ (1-19)

A mirror seems to be just like the image reflecting within
—it appears identical to the reflection shining within it—

but it also has a reality apart from that image,
independent and outside of that reflection.
In the same way the Supreme-Self
—that pervades all of existence and shines as the universe—
abides also as an independent entity.
That same entity shines inside the body as a body,
and also independently as the Supreme,
outside of the body.

एकं सर्वगतं व्योम बहिरन्तर्यथा घटे ।
ekaṁ sarvagataṁ vyoma bahirantaryathā ghaṭe ,
नित्यं निरन्तरं ब्रह्म सर्वभूतगणे तथा ॥ १-२० ॥
nityaṁ nirantaraṁ brahma sarvabhūtagaṇe tathā (1-20)

Just as the one all-permeating space pervades everywhere
—within the jar and outside too,
extending through all of things;
even so the eternal, everlasting Brahama-Rāma
exists throughout,
pervading the entirety of Existence.

:: End Canto – I ::

:: Canto – II ::
- Reveling as the Ātmā -

जनक उवाच
janaka uvāca:

अहो निरञ्जनः शान्तो बोधोऽहं प्रकृतेः परः ।
aho nirañjanaḥ śānto bodho'haṁ prakṛteḥ paraḥ ,
एतावन्तमहं कालं मोहेनैव विडम्बितः ॥२-१॥
etāvantamahaṁ kālaṁ mohenaiva viḍambitaḥ (2-1)

Janaka said:
Here I am:
a taintless awareness in perfect peace,
a pristine consciousness
undisturbed by any of nature's doings.
Imagine! All this time I had been deceived
by the delusive plays of Māyā—
Aho! How silly of me!

यथा प्रकाशयाम्येको देहमेनं तथा जगत् ।
yathā prakāśayāmyeko dehamenaṁ tathā jagat ,
अतो मम जगत्सर्वमथवा न च किञ्चन ॥२-२॥
ato mama jagatsarvamathavā na ca kiñcana (2-2)

It is only my Ātmā illuming all of this.
Only in the light of my consciousness
does this body stand revealed
—together with the rest of the universe.
So then,
not just this body,
isn't the entire universe me too?
...or perhaps none of either is!

स शरीरमहो विश्वं परित्यज्य मयाधुना ।
sa śarīramaho viśvaṁ parityajya mayādhunā ,
कुतश्चित् कौशलाद् एव परमात्मा विलोक्यते ॥२-३॥
kutaścit kauśalād eva paramātmā vilokyate (2-3)

Indeed! By dint of some ability,
now that I have left the body and the universe behind,
the Singularity of Param-Ātmā-Rāma becomes so clearly apparent to me—
so singularly real and tangible.

यथा न तोयतो भिन्नास्तरङ्गाः फेनबुद्बुदाः ।
yathā na toyato bhinnāstaraṅgāḥ phenabudbudāḥ ,
आत्मनो न तथा भिन्नं विश्वमात्मविनिर्गतम् ॥ २-४ ॥
ātmano na tathā bhinnaṁ viśvamātmavinirgatam (2-4)

Just as
the waves, foam, and bubbles
are identical to the water of which they are made,
even so this seemingly real universe
has emanated from the Param-Ātmā,
and is none other than the Ātmā
—my Self.

तन्तुमात्रो भवेद् एव पटो यद्वद् विचारितः ।
tantumātro bhaved eva paṭo yadvad vicāritaḥ ,
आत्मतन्मात्रमेवेदं तद्वद् विश्वं विचारितम् ॥ २-५ ॥
ātmatanmātramevedaṁ tadvad viśvaṁ vicāritam (2-5)

When examined closely,
the cloth is just the individual threads
and nothing but the threads;
even so
when I take apart this universe
—when I subject it to my dispassionate enquiry—
I find it comprised of nothing but the Ātmā-Rāma:
my Self.

यथैवेक्षुरसे क्लृप्ता तेन व्याप्तैव शर्करा ।
yathaivekṣurase klṛptā tena vyāptaiva śarkarā ,
तथा विश्वं मयि क्लृप्तं मया व्याप्तं निरन्तरम् ॥ २-६ ॥
tathā viśvaṁ mayi klṛptaṁ mayā vyāptaṁ nirantaram (2-6)

Just as the taste of sugarcane-juice
becomes diffused throughout the sugar
which got produced from that juice;
even so the universe
—crystallized out of my Self—
is pervaded with the essence of my Self
through and through.

आत्मज्ञानाज्जगद् भाति आत्मज्ञानान्न भासते ।
ātmajñānājjagad bhāti ātmajñānānna bhāsate ,
रज्ज्वज्ञानादहिर्भाति तज्ज्ञानाद् भासते न हि ॥२-७॥
rajjvajñānādahirbhāti tajjñānād bhāsate na hi (2-7)

Due to Nescience
—staying ignorant of the Ātmā—
the world appears to be Real;
and by the knowledge of the Ātmā
—in the effulgence of its fiery glow—
the delusive world vanishes forthwith.
This is just how a snake seemingly 'appears' within a rope in darkness;
and then 'disappears' into that same rope
when the light appears.

प्रकाशो मे निजं रूपं नातिरिक्तोऽस्म्यहं ततः ।
prakāśo me nijaṁ rūpaṁ nātirikto'smyahaṁ tataḥ ,
यदा प्रकाशते विश्वं तदाहं भास एव हि ॥२-८॥
yadā prakāśate viśvaṁ tadāhaṁ bhāsa eva hi (2-8)

My innate essence is a Fiery Light—
and other than the effulgence of Consciousness
I am nothing else.
When the universe shines forth,
it does so borrowing the glow of my brilliance.
Through and through everything which is manifest anywhere,
there is nothing except for the Fiery Ātmā
shining all splendorous.

अहो विकल्पितं विश्वमज्ञानान्मयि भासते ।
aho vikalpitaṁ viśvamajñānānmayi bhāsate ,
रूप्यं शुक्तौ फणी रज्जौ वारि सूर्यकरे यथा ॥२-९॥
rūpyaṁ śuktau phaṇī rajjau vāri sūryakare yathā (2-9)

Aho!
This universe
—conceived in me, wrought out by Nescience—
is a seeming appearance
...alike the shells scattered on a beach
which are imagined to be silver due to greed;
...or alike a rope which becomes visible as snake,
from out of fear of darkness;
...or like the "water" of mirage seen to be real due to the deluding heat of desert.

मत्तो विनिर्गतं विश्वं मय्येव लयमेष्यति ।
matto vinirgataṁ viśvaṁ mayyeva layameṣyati ,
मृदि कुम्भो जले वीचिः कनके कटकं यथा ॥२-१०॥
mṛdi kumbho jale vīciḥ kanake kaṭakaṁ yathā (2-10)

All this here, emerges out of me;
it exists in me;
and within me again
it becomes dissolved
—like an earthen jar returning to its
component clay,
...or a wave
blending back into the water again,
...or a gold bracelet
melting into the pureness of its element
—having become bereft of form
bereft of name.

अहो अहं नमो मह्यं विनाशो यस्य नास्ति मे ।
aho ahaṁ namo mahyaṁ vināśo yasya nāsti me ,
ब्रह्मादिस्तम्बपर्यन्तं जगन्नाशोऽपि तिष्ठतः ॥२-११॥
brahmādistambaparyantaṁ jagannāśo'pi tiṣṭhataḥ (2-11)

Aho! How grand!
Salutations to 'me'—
of whom there is never any destruction—
who always abide undestroyed unaffected—
who endures unabated even after destruction of the last manifestation.

After the whole universe
—from the god Brahammā down to a tiny straw—
go vanishing without a trace,
'I', the Ātmā,
still remain.

अहो अहं नमो मह्यमेकोऽहं देहवानपि ।
aho ahaṁ namo mahyameko'haṁ dehavānapi ,
क्वचिन्न गन्ता नागन्ता व्याप्य विश्वमवस्थितः ॥२-१२॥
kvacinna gantā nāgantā vyāpya viśvamavasthitaḥ (2-12)

Salutations to my Self, the Ātmā:
the One without a second,
the sole entity,
one that abides motionless
neither coming nor going
...although seemingly being borne alongside the body;
Aho! Glory to my soul—
forever existent
pervading the entirety of Existence.

अहो अहं नमो मह्यं दक्षो नास्तीह मत्समः ।
aho ahaṁ namo mahyaṁ dakṣo nāstīha matsamaḥ ,
असंस्पृश्य शरीरेण येन विश्वं चिरं धृतम् ॥२-१३॥
asaṁspṛśya śarīreṇa yena viśvaṁ ciraṁ dhṛtam (2-13)

Aho! Salutations to my Self, the Ātmā,
the like of whom there is no other!
Say who is so able as 'I'—
who have supported and carried aloft this entirety of existence
from all of eternity,
without even touching it with a finger!

अहो अहं नमो मह्यं यस्य मे नास्ति किञ्चन ।
aho ahaṁ namo mahyaṁ yasya me nāsti kiñcana ,
अथवा यस्य मे सर्वं यद् वाङ्मनसगोचरम् ॥ २-१४ ॥
athavā yasya me sarvaṁ yad vāṅmanasagocaram (2-14)

Aho, how wondrous!
Salutations to my Self
who possesses nothing at all
—or then again possesses everything that has been thought or spoken of
in the range of human thought
...and way beyond.

ज्ञानं ज्ञेयं तथा ज्ञाता त्रितयं नास्ति वास्तवम् ।
jñānaṁ jñeyaṁ tathā jñātā tritayaṁ nāsti vāstavam ,
अज्ञानाद् भाति यत्रेदं सोऽहमस्मि निरञ्जनः ॥ २-१५ ॥
ajñānād bhāti yatredaṁ so'hamasmi nirañjanaḥ (2-15)

The knower, the knowable, and its knowledge—
these three divisions do not really exist separated.
These have come to take distinct appearances in me
by dint of Māyā's play—
made feasible because of my ignorance of the Self.
In truth, I am the pristine Reality
—the One, the Ātmā—
in whom there is no distinction
of knower, knowledge, knowable, this, that.

द्वैतमूलमहो दुःखं नान्यत्तस्याऽस्ति भेषजम् ।
dvaitamūlamaho duḥkhaṁ nānyattasyā'sti bheṣajam ,
दृश्यमेतन् मृषा सर्वमेकोऽहं चिद्रसोमलः ॥ २-१६ ॥
dṛśyametan mṛṣā sarvameko'haṁ cidrasomalaḥ (2-16)

The notion of duality
is at the root of all grief and misery.
There is no other cure for sorrow
except the realization of the Truth,
that
"There are no two here—it is all just One."

All this perceived multifariousness
is just an apparition,
and behind it all is just the One pristine Reality
void of defilements,
comprised of bliss and consciousness.

बोधमात्रोऽहमज्ञानाद् उपाधिः कल्पितो मया ।
bodhamātro'hamajñānād upādhiḥ kalpito mayā ,
एवं विमृशतो नित्यं निर्विकल्पे स्थितिर्मम ॥२-१७॥
evaṁ vimṛśato nityaṁ nirvikalpe sthitirmama (2-17)

"Verily I am a pure consciousness;
but suffering from the malady of Self-Ignorance
—oblivious of my Real essence—
I have visited limitations upon myself
—bonds, alas, of my own making!"
...reflecting thusly,
I ever abide in my true essence,
as one within the Supreme-Self.

न मे बन्धोऽस्ति मोक्षो वा भ्रान्तिः शान्तो निराश्रया ।
na me bandho'sti mokṣo vā bhrāntiḥ śānto nirāśrayā ,
अहो मयि स्थितं विश्वं वस्तुतो न मयि स्थितम् ॥२-१८॥
aho mayi sthitaṁ viśvaṁ vastuto na mayi sthitam (2-18)

In truth there are no bondages on me
—and consequently the idea of liberation for me has no relevance.
With the notions of duality fading away,
illusions for me have now ceased
...lost their footing.
Truly all that that exists,
exists just in 'me'
—the Non-dual, the Substratum, the Singularity—
although ultimately
all this does not even really exist, such as it seems to appear.

सशरीरमिदं विश्वं न किञ्चिदिति निश्चितम् ।
saśarīramidaṁ viśvaṁ na kiñciditi niścitam ,
शुद्धचिन्मात्र आत्मा च तत्कस्मिन् कल्पनाधुना ॥ २-१९ ॥
śuddhacinmātra ātmā ca tatkasmin kalpanādhunā (2-19)

I have realized the essence of myself
to be just the Self—the Ātmā, the pristine consciousness;
and now I know with all certainty
that this body and the universe
are all non-Real—non-abiding.
So now,
what thing is left for my mentations to build any fancies upon?
—for my thoughts to build any imaginations from?

शरीरं स्वर्गनरकौ बन्धमोक्षौ भयं तथा ।
śarīraṁ svarganarakau bandhamokṣau bhayaṁ tathā ,
कल्पनामात्रमेवैतत् किं मे कार्यं चिदात्मनः ॥ २-२० ॥
kalpanāmātramevaitat kiṁ me kāryaṁ cidātmanaḥ (2-20)

Body, bondages, freedom, heavens, hell
—and fear as well—
are mere ideations and imaginations of the mind.
What have I
—who am pure bliss and consciousness—
got to do with any of that?

अहो जनसमूहेऽपि न द्वैतं पश्यतो मम ।
aho janasamūhe'pi na dvaitaṁ paśyato mama ,
अरण्यमिव संवृत्तं क्व रतिं करवाण्यहम् ॥ २-२१ ॥
araṇyamiva saṁvṛttaṁ kva ratiṁ karavāṇyaham (2-21)

Aho! In my sight
there is no longer any duality seen!!
Even this throng of multitudes
—the apparent 'this here' and 'there that',
and the 'you-and-me's—
appears like a blurry cornucopia,
a smudged out faraway wilderness.

Other than the Ātmā
what else really exists that I can possibly
pleasure from? ...become engaged with?

नाहं देहो न मे देहो जीवो नाहमहं हि चित् ।
nāhaṁ deho na me deho jīvo nāhamahaṁ hi cit ,
अयमेव हि मे बन्ध आसीद्या जीविते स्पृहा ॥२-२२॥
ayameva hi me bandha āsīdyā jīvite spṛhā (2-22)

I am not this body
—and nor had I ever a body—
I am not the Jīva,
I am nothing but a Pure Consciousness.
This indeed was my bondage:
that I once had this 'me' and 'mine';
and that I thirsted for life
in greed, desires, covetousness;
and that I fancied little bites of joys
—while in fact
the entire ocean of bliss was just I myself.

अहो भुवनकल्लोलैर्विचित्रैर्द्राक् समुत्थितम् ।
aho bhuvanakallolairvicitrairdrāk samutthitam ,
मय्यनन्तमहाम्भोधौ चित्तवाते समुद्यते ॥२-२३॥
mayyanantamahāmbhodhau cittavāte samudyate (2-23)

Aho!
In this limitless Ocean of my Consciousness,
I sometimes find these little worldly waves
—diverse, colorful, variegated—
—rising and falling—
impelled simply by the currents of my imaginations.

मय्यनन्तमहाम्भोधौ चित्तवाते प्रशाम्यति ।
mayyanantamahāmbhodhau cittavāte praśāmyati ,
अभाग्याज्जीववणिजो जगत्पोतो विनश्वरः ॥२-२४॥
abhāgyājjīvavaṇijo jagatpoto vinaśvaraḥ (2-24)

In the infinite ocean of my Self,
when the winds of the mind start to calm down then,
the ark of the universe
begins to sink ...sink, ...sink away
...meeting its destruction
—which becomes rather calamitous
for the Jīva (soul):
who is the anserine bedazed merchant sitting in that ark
carrying on his greedy trades with the world there.

मय्यनन्तमहाम्भोधावाश्चर्यं जीववीचयः ।
mayyanantamahāmbhodhāvāścaryaṁ jīvavīcayaḥ ,
उद्यन्ति घ्नन्ति खेलन्ति प्रविशन्ति स्वभावतः ॥२-२५॥
udyanti ghnanti khelanti praviśanti svabhāvataḥ (2-25)

Aho, how marvelous!
In me,
the seamless ocean without an end,
waves after waves
—of beings and things—
arise,
and they collide and commingle,
...and they play for a little while
—propelled by their innate traits—
...and then suddenly
...they all vanish away without a trace.

:: End Canto – II ::

:: Canto – III ::
- Veracity of Self-Realization -

अष्टावक्र उवाच
aṣṭāvakra uvāca:

अविनाशिनमात्मानमेकं विज्ञाय तत्त्वतः ।
avināśinamātmānamekaṁ vijñāya tattvataḥ ,
तवात्मज्ञानस्य धीरस्य कथमर्थार्जने रतिः ॥ ३-१ ॥
tavātmajñānasya dhīrasya kathamarthārjane ratiḥ (3-1)

Ashtāvakra said:
Once having known the Self to be
one's own imperishable eternal essence
—and if you stand established in that knowledge—
how can it be that you shall feel fondness for acquiring wealth
—you who are the knower of the Self,
perfect and complete in all your fullness?

[This Canto III enumerates the Tests of Self-Realization. How far one has progressed on the path of Self-Realization, may be gauged by examining oneself against these verses.]

आत्माज्ञानादहो प्रीतिर्विषयभ्रमगोचरे ।
ātmājñānādaho prītirviṣayabhramagocare ,
शुक्तेरज्ञानतो लोभो यथा रजतविभ्रमे ॥ ३-२ ॥
śukterajñānato lobho yathā rajatavibhrame (3-2)

When one is bereft of Self-Realization
—when one is bound in Ignorance,
when one lives forgetful of one's true nature—
then only do deluding notions
—such as hatred and fondness ... and what not—
arise alongside sense perceptions.
Sometimes at the beach, a feeling of greed arises for the deluding "silver found!"
—as long as the truth of the mother-of-pearl
remains unknown due to Ignorance.
Similarly,
towards the beings and things of the universe
—seen to be some "enchanting others!",

on account of the ignorance of the One-Nondual-Reality—
greed, desires etc., emotions
arise in the deluded mind.

विश्वं स्फुरति यत्रेदं तरङ्गा इव सागरे ।
viśvaṁ sphurati yatredaṁ taraṅgā iva sāgare ,
सोऽहमस्मीति विज्ञाय किं दीन इव धावसि ॥ ३-३ ॥
so'hamasmīti vijñāya kiṁ dīna iva dhāvasi (3-3)

"That Infinite Ocean of Consciousness
—in whom this universe is effervescing and wavering
like rising-falling waves undulating in a sea—
verily I am that Supreme-Being,"
recognizing the veracity of this Truth,
why do you run about in the world like an abject being?
...an object of contempt and pity?

श्रुत्वापि शुद्धचैतन्य आत्मानमतिसुन्दरं ।
śrutvāpi śuddhacaitanya ātmānamatisundaraṁ ,
उपस्थेऽत्यन्तसंसक्तो मालिन्यमधिगच्छति ॥ ३-४ ॥
upasthe'tyantasaṁsakto mālinyamadhigacchati (3-4)

Having heard of the Truth
—and having directly realized one's Self to be that pristine
Consciousness of surpassing beauty—
how can one still go about lusting
after sordid sexual things?
...continue to dwell
in the embrace of impurity?

सर्वभूतेषु चात्मानं सर्वभूतानि चात्मनि ।
sarvabhūteṣu cātmānaṁ sarvabhūtāni cātmani ,
मुनेर्जानत आश्चर्यं ममत्वमनुवर्तते ॥ ३-५ ॥
munerjānata āścaryaṁ mamatvamanuvartate (3-5)

He who has realized the Self in all,
and everything in the Self
—in that wise sage,
it would be most strange
if the impressions of ownership and separation

—the sense of 'me', 'you', 'mine', 'this', 'that'—
should still continue unabated
just as before.

आस्थितः परमाद्वैतं मोक्षार्थेऽपि व्यवस्थितः ।
āsthitaḥ paramādvaitaṁ mokṣārthe'pi vyavasthitaḥ ,
आश्चर्यं कामवशगो विकलः केलिशिक्षया ॥ ३-६ ॥
āścaryaṁ kāmavaśago vikalaḥ keliśikṣayā (3-6)

With *Moksha* as the supreme goal
—to become one within the Absolute One—
he who is completely engaged in merging within
the Singularity—the Param-Ātmā,
it would be passing strange,
if one would yet remain a slave to his desires,
still let himself be subjugated by lust,
still allow himself to be weakened
in the practices of amorous pastimes!

उद्भूतं ज्ञानदुर्मित्रमवधार्यातिदुर्बलः ।
udbhūtaṁ jñānadurmitramavadhāryātidurbalaḥ ,
आश्चर्यं काममाकाङ्क्षेत् कालमन्तमनुश्रितः ॥ ३-७ ॥
āścaryaṁ kāmamākāṅkṣet kālamantamanuśritaḥ (3-7)

It would be most strange if he
—who knows lust to be the dire enemy of wisdom,
who is already much debilitated from pandering to cravings
spanning an entire lifetime—
that man would still be eager as ever
for yet more sweet sensual encounters...
even though hearing the footsteps of death
draw near and nearer,
with every passing second.

इहामुत्र विरक्तस्य नित्यानित्यविवेकिनः ।
ihāmutra viraktasya nityānityavivekinaḥ ,
आश्चर्यं मोक्षकामस्य मोक्षाद् एव विभीषिका ॥ ३-८ ॥
āścaryaṁ mokṣakāmasya mokṣād eva vibhīṣikā (3-8)

It would be passing strange if he
—who is un-attached to things of this world and the afterworld
—who discriminates
between the eternal and the ephemeral
(the Real and the non-Real)
—and who aspires for Liberation
...should still be afraid of losing individuality
...should yet fear the dissolution of his body
to merge within the Infinite!

धीरस्तु भोज्यमानोऽपि पीड्यमानोऽपि सर्वदा ।
dhīrastu bhojyamāno'pi pīḍyamāno'pi sarvadā ,
आत्मानं केवलं पश्यन् न तुष्यति न कुप्यति ॥ ३-९ ॥
ātmānaṁ kevalaṁ paśyan na tuṣyati na kupyati (3-9)

Whether feted or beset at times,
and whether tormented or regaled,
the steadfast wise sage perceives just the
One-Absolute-Self disporting in the world;
and he ever abides of a serene countenance
—neither enthralled,
nor ever enraged.

चेष्टमानं शरीरं स्वं पश्यत्यन्यशरीरवत् ।
ceṣṭamānaṁ śarīraṁ svaṁ paśyatyanyaśarīravat ,
संस्तवे चापि निन्दायां कथं क्षुभ्येत् महाशयः ॥ ३-१० ॥
saṁstave cāpi nindāyāṁ kathaṁ kṣubhyet mahāśayaḥ (3-10)

The exalted sage,
even while witnessing the enactments of his own person,
sees them as if they were a distant occurrence
—of someone else's.
Can such a one ever be perturbed
when subjected to praise or blame?

मायामात्रमिदं विश्वं पश्यन् विगतकौतुकः ।
māyāmātramidaṁ viśvaṁ paśyan vigatakautukaḥ ,
अपि सन्निहिते मृत्यौ कथं त्रस्यति धीरधीः ॥ ३-११ ॥
api sannihite mṛtyau kathaṁ trasyati dhīradhīḥ (3-11)

Aloof and unconcerned
—seeing this world as the drama of Rāma's Māyā,
with interest departed from any of His plays—
how can the steady minded sage tremble
hearing the beats of Kāla (Time)?
... fear the approaching footsteps of Death?

निःस्पृहं मानसं यस्य नैराश्येऽपि महात्मनः ।
niḥspṛhaṁ mānasaṁ yasya nairāśye'pi mahātmanaḥ ,
तस्यात्मज्ञानतृप्तस्य तुलना केन जायते ॥३-१२॥
tasyātmajñānatṛptasya tulanā kena jāyate (3-12)

He
—who in his Realization
abides completely identified with the Supreme-Self
—whose joys abide all within
—in whom arise no wishful thinkings even amidst disappointments,
—who has no desires left...
not even the desire to become utterly desireless
—such a one is a true sage
...and who can really compare to that exalted one?

स्वभावाद् एव जानानो दृश्यमेतन्न किञ्चन ।
svabhāvād eva jānāno dṛśyametanna kiñcana ,
इदं ग्राह्यमिदं त्याज्यं स किं पश्यति धीरधीः ॥३-१३॥
idaṁ grāhyamidaṁ tyājyaṁ sa kiṁ paśyati dhīradhīḥ (3-13)

Unto that steady-minded-sage,
what is fit? ...and what unfit?
For he knows all objects of perceptions to be void of Realness
when examined at their essence
—because all existence is simply Brahama.
In him, the distinctions of the Seer and the Seen stand dissolved naturally.
What would cause him to weigh in
on the merits or demerits of things?
... as 'this is acceptable' and 'not this'?

अन्तस्त्यक्तकषायस्य निर्द्वन्द्वस्य निराशिषः ।
antastyaktakaṣāyasya nirdvandvasya nirāśiṣaḥ ,
यदृच्छयागतो भोगो न दुःखाय न तुष्टये ॥ ३-१४॥
yadṛcchayāgato bhogo na duḥkhāya na tuṣṭaye (3-14)

Unto the inwardly renunciant
—who has foresworn all worldly interest from within—
when something to be partaken is placed before
—good or bad, that which has come of its own accord—
then it makes up for neither delight nor pain for him
—because he has already eliminated all attachments;
and abides he
void of all dualistic notions
...freed of joys ...freed of sorrows.

:: End Canto – III ::

:: Canto – IV ::
- Glory of Self-Realization -

जनक उवाच
janaka uvāca:

हन्तात्मज्ञानस्य धीरस्य खेलतो भोगलीलया ।
hantātmajñānasya dhīrasya khelato bhogalīlayā ,
न हि संसारवाहीकैर्मूढैः सह समानता ॥४-१॥
na hi saṁsāravāhīkairmūḍhaiḥ saha samānatā (4-1)

Janaka said:
The sage,
possessed of self-knowledge,
who remains established in the Ātmā,
who is found merely disporting in life
living just for the enjoyment of the show
—which to him is mere play—
bears no resemblance whatsoever to the deluded fools of the world:
beasts of burden piteously hauling burdensome carts of life,
made heavy and overflowing with worldly objects,
amassed for sense-pleasures.

यत् पदं प्रेप्सवो दीनाः शक्राद्याः सर्वदेवताः ।
yat padaṁ prepsavo dīnāḥ śakrādyāḥ sarvadevatāḥ ,
अहो तत्र स्थितो योगी न हर्षमुपगच्छति ॥४-२॥
aho tatra sthito yogī na harṣamupagacchati (4-2)

Even suffering the state of mirthful revelries
—those ravishing spheres of pleasures which even gods like Indra yearn for disconsolately—
the yogi finds no excitement existing in them
—being that he always abides
in That-Ocean-of-Bliss
where such morsels of delights
are but tiny fleeting waves
...flapping away

तज्ज्ञस्य पुण्यपापाभ्यां स्पर्शो ह्यन्तर्न जायते ।
tajjñasya puṇyapāpābhyāṁ sparśo hyantarna jāyate ,
न ह्याकाशस्य धूमेन दृश्यमानापि सङ्गतिः ॥४-३॥
na hyākāśasya dhūmena dṛśyamānāpi saṅgatiḥ (4-3)

Having intimately known and touched the very realm of the Absolute
—pristine and bereft of taints—
the yogi remains untouched of virtue and vice,
of all deeds good and bad
—just as the sky remains untouched by smoke,
however much it may appear to overwhelm.

आत्मैवेदं जगत्सर्वं ज्ञातं येन महात्मना ।
ātmaivedaṁ jagatsarvaṁ jñātaṁ yena mahātmanā ,
यदृच्छया वर्तमानं तं निषेद्धुं क्षमेत कः ॥४-४॥
yadṛcchayā vartamānaṁ taṁ niṣeddhuṁ kṣameta kaḥ (4-4)

Who or what really can prevent that exalted sage
—he who has known the entire universe to be only the Ātmā—
from disporting as he well chooses to?
...from carrying on spontaneously in
the flow of the moment?
...from going wheresoever his heart bids?

आब्रह्मस्तम्बपर्यन्ते भूतग्रामे चतुर्विधे ।
ābrahmastambaparyante bhūtagrāme caturvidhe ,
विज्ञस्यैव हि सामर्थ्यमिच्छानिच्छाविवर्जने ॥४-५॥
vijñasyaiva hi sāmarthyamicchānicchāvivarjane (4-5)

Of the four kinds of created beings
—from little tufts of green up to the highest god: Brahammā—
it is only the man possessed of knowledge
—one who has realized the Self,
who has risen above the waves of dualities—
who is capable of standing tall over feelings of the hearts
...transcend aversions and desires.

आत्मानमद्वयं कश्चिज्जानाति जगदीश्वरम् ।
ātmānamadvayaṁ kaścijjānāti jagadīśvaram ,
यद् वेत्ति तत्स कुरुते न भयं तस्य कुत्रचित् ॥ ४-६ ॥
yad vetti tatsa kurute na bhayaṁ tasya kutracit (4-6)

He who has realized himself as One with The-One
—the non-dual Totality, the Supreme-Self,
the undivided Lord of the world—
rare indeed is that human
found walking here on earth.
Disporting through life,
completely free,
he simply does what he does
—and has no fear from any quarter.

:: End Canto – IV ::

:: Canto – V ::
- Dissolution -

अष्टावक्र उवाच
aṣṭāvakra uvāca:

न ते सङ्गोऽस्ति केनापि किं शुद्धस्त्यक्तुमिच्छसि ।
na te saṅgo'sti kenāpi kiṁ śuddhastyaktumicchasi ,
सङ्घातविलयं कुर्वन्नेवमेव लयं व्रज ॥५-१॥
saṅghātavilayaṁ kurvannevameva layaṁ vraja (5-1)

Ashtāvakra said:
There is nothing at all here attached to which you lie bound in fetters.
Pure and taintless you already are—
so what is that you must needs give up?
Renounce simply the idea of a body—
set aside this composite organism to rest.
Give up identifying yourself with this assemblage of skin, bone, organs.
Abide dissolved,
knowing that you are not anything material
but the Ātmā pure.

उदेति भवतो विश्वं वारिधेरिव बुद्बुदः ।
udeti bhavato viśvaṁ vāridheriva budbudaḥ ,
इति ज्ञात्वैकमात्मानमेवमेव लयं व्रज ॥५-२॥
iti jñātvaikamātmānamevameva layaṁ vraja (5-2)

"This universe arises in Me
just like waves and bubbles foaming out of the sea"
—having known yourself to be That
—knowing your Self to be pegged within That Supreme-Self—
enter the State of Dissolution:
that of Oneness within the Param-Ātmā-Rāma.

प्रत्यक्षमप्यवस्तुत्वाद् विश्वं नास्त्यमले त्वयि ।
pratyakṣamapyavastutvād viśvaṁ nāstyamale tvayi ,
रज्जुसर्प इव व्यक्तमेवमेव लयं व्रज ॥५-३॥
rajjusarpa iva vyaktamevameva layaṁ vraja (5-3)

Although perceived to be Real,
all this which rises in front of your eyes,
is really non-Real
—because everything is rushing forward to meet their own destructive end,
to become rendered into a naught once again with time.
Only the immaculate pure Consciousness
—bereft of the taints of perceptions—
is the real you: the Reality that never dies.
Like a snake imagined in rope,
the universe is an apparition
—know this Truth and return home.
Meld dissolved,
back into the Reality where you really belong.

समदुःखसुखः पूर्ण आशानैराश्ययोः समः ।
samaduḥkhasukhaḥ pūrṇa āśānairāśyayoḥ samaḥ ,
समजीवितमृत्युः सन्नेवमेव लयं व्रज ॥५-४॥
samajīvitamṛtyuḥ sannevameva layaṁ vraja (5-4)

In sorrows and in delights,
in hope and despair,
in births and deaths,
in living and in dying
—ever remain equanimous.
By dint of your oneness in That-Supreme-One,
you already are perfect and complete
...in lack of nothing.
Therefore realizing that
you are the Ātmā in the Param-Ātmā,
enter the State of Dissolution
...within that Supreme-Self.

:: End Canto – V ::

:: Canto – VI ::
- Supreme Truth -

जनक उवाच
janaka uvāca:

आकाशवदनन्तोऽहं घटवत् प्राकृतं जगत् ।
ākāśavadananto'haṁ ghaṭavat prākṛtaṁ jagat ,
इति ज्ञानं तथैतस्य न त्यागो न ग्रहो लयः ॥६-१॥
iti jñānaṁ tathaitasya na tyāgo na graho layaḥ (6-1)

Janaka said:
"I am like the boundless infinite Space-Time,
and this phenomenal world is like some jar existing in a little space for a little while,"
—this annunciation encapsulates
the Supreme Truth.
And That Highest Truth
—that ever-abiding Ocean-of-Consciousness—
can neither be given up,
nor taken up,
nor uncreated;
it is the only existent Reality,
rest all is false.

महोदधिरिवाहं स प्रपञ्चो वीचिसऽन्निभः ।
mahodadhirivāhaṁ sa prapañco vīcisa'nnibhaḥ ,
इति ज्ञानं तथैतस्य न त्यागो न ग्रहो लयः ॥६-२॥
iti jñānaṁ tathaitasya na tyāgo na graho layaḥ (6-2)

"I am an Ocean of Consciousness;
and this universe of multiplicity is like
the varicolored waves undulating within It,"
—this aforesaid is the Truth of Reality
which stands by dint of its own veracity;
and of that Reality
there is neither rejection,
nor acceptance, nor dissolution.

अहं स शुक्तिसङ्काशो रूप्यवद् विश्वकल्पना ।
aham sa śuktisaṅkāśo rūpyavad viśvakalpanā ,
इति ज्ञानं तथैतस्य न त्यागो न ग्रहो लयः ॥६-३॥
iti jñānaṁ tathaitasya na tyāgo na graho layaḥ (6-3)

"I am the reality of mother-of-pearl,
and the illusion of the universe is like the silver imagined in that nacre"
—this is the Truth of the Self and Universe;
and of that Truth,
renunciation, embracement, or negation of it
has simply no meaning.

अहं वा सर्वभूतेषु सर्वभूतान्यथो मयि ।
aham vā sarvabhūteṣu sarvabhūtānyatho mayi ,
इति ज्ञानं तथैतस्य न त्यागो न ग्रहो लयः ॥६-४॥
iti jñānaṁ tathaitasya na tyāgo na graho layaḥ (6-4)

"I am in all beings, and all beings exist in me"
—this is the Truth of the Reality of Consciousness;
and any ideas of rejection, or acceptance, or denial of that Reality is irrelevant and meaningless.
That Supreme Truth, that Reality,
stands purely by Itself,
needing no other validation.

:: End Canto – VI ::

:: Canto – VII ::
- Describing Self-Realization -

जनक उवाच
janaka uvāca:

मय्यनन्तमहाम्भोधौ विश्वपोत इतस्ततः ।
mayyanantamahāmbhodhau viśvapota itastataḥ ,
भ्रमति स्वान्तवातेन न ममास्त्यसहिष्णुता ॥७-१॥
bhramati svāntavātena na mamāstyasahiṣṇutā (7-1)

Janaka said:
In Me
—the Boundless-Ocean-of-Consciousness—
the Ark of the Universe moves hither thither,
propelled by the winds of Māyā
—driven by the innate nature of things—
and I am not in the least
disturbed by any of it.

मय्यनन्तमहाम्भोधौ जगद्वीचिः स्वभावतः ।
mayyanantamahāmbhodhau jagadvīciḥ svabhāvataḥ ,
उदेतु वास्तमायातु न मे वृद्धिर्न च क्षतिः ॥७-२॥
udetu vāstamāyātu na me vṛddhirna ca kṣatiḥ (7-2)

In the infinite Ocean of my Self,
I see the waves of the universe
rising and falling of themselves;
let it be;
what is all that to me?
I am neither raised nor diminished
by any of it.

मय्यनन्तमहाम्भोधौ विश्वं नाम विकल्पना ।
mayyanantamahāmbhodhau viśvaṁ nāma vikalpanā ,
अतिशान्तो निराकार एतदेवाहमास्थितः ॥७-३॥
atiśānto nirākāra etadevāhamāsthitaḥ (7-3)

Although in the infinite Ocean of my Self,
this phantasma of the universe has risen
—like evanescing waves in unceasing pulsations—
I, as the Ātmā, abide in supreme peace
—formless and tranquil, bereft of attributes and tarnishes—
and I always abide as such only.

नात्मा भावेषु नो भावस्तत्रानन्ते निरञ्जने ।
nātmā bhāveṣu no bhāvastatrānante nirañjane ,
इत्यसक्तोऽस्पृहः शान्त एतदेवाहमास्तितः ॥ ७-४ ॥
ityasakto'spṛhaḥ śānta etadevāhamāstitaḥ (7-4)

The essence of the limitless stainless perfect Self
—which I am—
cannot be captured in any manifested object.
I am the infinite Ātmā
—ever-tranquil unconfined unattached lustless—
and only as That Matterless Unmanifest-Reality
I do ever abide.

अहो चिन्मात्रमेवाहमिन्द्रजालोपमं जगत् ।
aho cinmātramevāhamindrajālopamaṁ jagat ,
इति मम कथं कुत्र हेयोपादेयकल्पना ॥ ७-५ ॥
iti mama kathaṁ kutra heyopādeyakalpanā (7-5)

Truly I am only the Absolute Consciousness,
and this world is like a magic show playing before the eyes.
Knowing all this to be an illusion,
what need have I
to be in acceptance or denial of any of that?

:: End Canto – VII ::

:: Canto – VIII ::
- Bondage and Liberation -

अष्टावक्र उवाच
aṣṭāvakra uvāca:

तदा बन्धो यदा चित्तं किञ्चिद् वाञ्छति शोचति ।
tadā bandho yadā cittaṁ kiñcid vāñchati śocati ,
किञ्चिन् मुञ्चति गृण्हाति किञ्चिद् दृष्यति कुप्यति ॥८-१॥
kiñcin muñcati gṛṇhāti kiñcid dṛṣyati kupyati (8-1)

Ashtāvakra said:
When the mind desires,
when the mind grieves,
when it accepts or rejects anything,
when it feels elated or dejected or angered over something
—all that is bondage.
Verily all bondages are only of the mind!

तदा मुक्तिर्यदा चित्तं न वाञ्छति न शोचति ।
tadā muktiryadā cittaṁ na vāñchati na śocati ,
न मुञ्चति न गृण्हाति न हृष्यति न कुप्यति ॥८-२॥
na muñcati na gṛṇhāti na hṛṣyati na kupyati (8-2)

Liberation is:
when the mind does not crave after anything,
when it does not grieve over anything,
when it does not cling to anything,
when it is not pleased or displeased
about anything.
Aye, liberation is when the mind rests dissolved.

तदा बन्धो यदा चित्तं सक्तं काश्वपि दृष्टिषु ।
tadā bandho yadā cittaṁ saktaṁ kāśvapi dṛṣṭiṣu ,
तदा मोक्षो यदा चित्तमसक्तं सर्वदृष्टिषु ॥८-३॥
tadā mokṣo yadā cittamasaktaṁ sarvadṛṣṭiṣu (8-3)

When the mind is attached to sense-organs and memories
—that causes Bondage;
and the very obverse is Liberation
—when the mind remains untangled from all sense experiences...
past, present,
or future expectations.

यदा नाहं तदा मोक्षो यदाहं बन्धनं तदा ।
yadā nāhaṁ tadā mokṣo yadāhaṁ bandhanaṁ tadā ,
मत्वेति हेलया किञ्चिन्मा गृहाण विमुञ्च मा ॥८-४॥
matveti helayā kiñcinmā gṛhāṇa vimuñca mā (8-4)

When there is no more 'me' and 'mine'
—that is Liberation;
and where there arises 'me' and 'mine'
—that forthwith engenders Bondage.
Reflect on this diligently
and then
neither embrace, nor abhor
—simply eliminate the notions of 'me' and 'mine' from within,
and let simply spontaneity have her play.

:: End Canto – VIII ::

:: Canto – IX ::
- Aloofness -

अष्टावक्र उवाच
aṣṭāvakra uvāca:

कृताकृते च द्वन्द्वानि कदा शान्तानि कस्य वा ।
kṛtākṛte ca dvandvāni kadā śāntāni kasya vā ,
एवं ज्ञात्वेह निर्वेदाद् भव त्यागपरोऽव्रती ॥९-१॥
evaṁ jñātveha nirvedād bhava tyāgaparo'vratī (9-1)

Ashtāvakra said:
Duties done ...and many more still left undone
...and the unceasing waves of worldly dualities
...and the pairs of opposites—
when, and for whom,
has this onerous procession of worldly affairs ever ceased?
Accepting this inevitability,
and abiding dispassionate and desireless
—intent on renunciation through a thorough indifference to the world—
embrace arrant Aloofness.

कस्यापि तात धन्यस्य लोकचेष्टावलोकनात् ।
kasyāpi tāta dhanyasya lokaceṣṭāvalokanāt ,
जीवितेच्छा बुभुक्षा च बुभुत्सोपशमः गताः ॥९-२॥
jīvitecchā bubhukṣā ca bubhutsopaśamaḥ gatāḥ (9-2)

O friend,
rare indeed is the blessed soul
whose keen insights
—from having observed the world and managing to learn from the experiences of others—
have lead him to the pristine shore of arrant Dispassion
—beyond the niggling thirst for living,
thirst for pleasures, thirst for knowing—
...where exists only an all-completeness,
a totality of Bliss.

अनित्यं सर्वमेवेदं तापत्रितयदूषितं ।
anityaṁ sarvamevedaṁ tāpatritayadūṣitaṁ ,
असारं निन्दितं हेयमिति निश्चित्य शाम्यति ॥९-३॥
asāraṁ ninditaṁ heyamiti niścitya śāmyati (9-3)

All that which men so urgently cling to,
...all that is impermanent brittle fragile,
easily spoilt in the wake of three-fold miseries of the world.
Recognizing the Seen to be deceptive and non-Real
—insubstantial and un-permanent, unworthy and unfit for acceptance—
the Seer acts accordingly and
—becoming aloof—
attains he to abiding peace.

कोऽसौ कालो वयः किं वा यत्र द्वन्द्वानि नो नृणाम् ।
ko'sau kālo vayaḥ kiṁ vā yatra dvandvāni no nṛṇām ,
तान्युपेक्ष्य यथाप्राप्तवर्ती सिद्धिमवाप्नुयात् ॥९-४॥
tānyupekṣya yathāprāptavartī siddhimavāpnuyāt (9-4)

When was a time
—and in which Age—
when the pairs of opposites have not existed in creation?
The world subsists by dint of dualities.
He who has gone beyond these in his heart
—content with whatever comes to happen by itself—
attains perfection
...through aloofness.

नाना मतं महर्षीणां साधूनां योगिनां तथा ।
nānā mataṁ maharṣīṇāṁ sādhūnāṁ yogināṁ tathā ,
दृष्ट्वा निर्वेदमापन्नः को न शाम्यति मानवः ॥९-५॥
dṛṣṭvā nirvedamāpannaḥ ko na śāmyati mānavaḥ (9-5)

Having observed such a diversity of opinions
even amongst august schools of sages, yogis,
and experts of the world,
what man is there
who does not become indifferent
to [the sham of] learning and scholarship?
Simply aim for quietude—
giving up this futile quest for learning so many divergent things.
Abide Aloof.

कृत्वा मूर्तिपरिज्ञानं चैतन्यस्य न किं गुरुः ।
kṛtvā mūrtiparijñānaṁ caitanyasya na kiṁ guruḥ ,
निर्वेदसमतायुक्त्या यस्तारयति संसृतेः ॥९-६॥
nirvedasamatāyuktyā yastārayati saṁsṛteḥ (9-6)

Isn't he a true spiritual guide
who has come by the knowledge of nature of Reality through reasoning and equanimity,
and by a stoical aloofness to the world;
...and who
—out of fullness of his heart—
is driven to enlighten others that may be hurting?

पश्य भूतविकारांस्त्वं भूतमात्रान् यथार्थतः ।
paśya bhūtavikārāṁstvaṁ bhūtamātrān yathārthataḥ ,
तत्क्षणाद् बन्धनिर्मुक्तः स्वरूपस्थो भविष्यसि ॥९-७॥
tatkṣaṇād bandhanirmuktaḥ svarūpastho bhaviṣyasi (9-7)

Abide Aloof.
If behind all changes occurring in the world
you see nothing but divergent elements in a relentless play
—acting, reacting, enacting
...driven by their essential nature—
then forthwith you shall stand freed of all bondages of the mind,
becoming established in your own innate essence instantly:
that of being the unfettered Ātmā pristine.

वासना एव संसार इति सर्वा विमुञ्च ताः ।
vāsanā eva saṁsāra iti sarvā vimuñca tāḥ ,
तत्त्यागो वासनात्यागात्स्थितिरद्य यथा तथा ॥९-८॥
tattyāgo vāsanātyāgātsthitiradya yathā tathā (9-8)

Vāsanā
—fondness, attachments, desires, 'me', 'mine'—
is what comprises the world.
Do therefore relinquish all Vāsanās from the mind.
Abide Aloof.
The renunciation of Vāsanās alone is true renunciation of the world.
Having first given those up,
then only can you dwell in the world unafraid
...anywhere.

:: End Canto – IX ::

:: Canto – X ::
- Equanimity -

अष्टावक्र उवाच
aṣṭāvakra uvāca:

विहाय वैरिणं काममर्थं चानर्थसङ्कुलम् ।
vihāya vairiṇaṁ kāmamarthaṁ cānarthasaṅkulam ,
धर्ममप्येतयोर्हेतुं सर्वत्रानादरं कुरु ॥ १०-१ ॥
dharmamapyetayorhetuṁ sarvatrānādaraṁ kuru (10-1)

Ashtāvakra said:
Recognize the arch enemy of Self-Realization to be Kāma and Artha
...and have nothing to do with them.
Kāma (desire for pleasures)
and Artha (propensity for worldly prosperity)
—are both fraught with evil;
abandon them as you will some toxic poison.
And finally be not a slave to Dharma either—
because it's from that again that they may all spring back to life.
Thus go beyond the three-fold human endeavors of Dharma, Artha, Kāma
...and forever embrace Equanimousness.

स्वप्नेन्द्रजालवत् पश्य दिनानि त्रीणि पञ्च वा ।
svapnendrajālavat paśya dināni trīṇi pañca vā ,
मित्रक्षेत्रधनागारदारदायादिसंपदः ॥ १०-२ ॥
mitrakṣetradhanāgāradāradāyādisaṁpadaḥ (10-2)

Look upon friends, possessions, riches, house, spouse, endowments and other marks of fortune
to be just like some passing dreams
—or show of a magic created by an illusionist—
which last for just a little while
...perhaps three days or five.
And always remain awake in Equanimity.

यत्र यत्र भवेत्तृष्णा संसारं विद्धि तत्र वै ।
yatra yatra bhavettṛṣṇā saṁsāraṁ viddhi tatra vai ,
प्रौढवैराग्यमाश्रित्य वीततृष्णः सुखी भव ॥ १०-३ ॥
prauḍhavairāgyamāśritya vītatṛṣṇaḥ sukhī bhava (10-3)

Know that whenever there arises even a single desire,
the whole world rises along with that.
Established in steadfast dispassion
—staunch and unwavering—
go past desiring,
and always remain happy.
Ever abide in Equanimity.

तृष्णामात्रात्मको बन्धस्तन्नाशो मोक्ष उच्यते ।
tṛṣṇāmātrātmako bandhastannāśo mokṣa ucyate ,
भवासंसक्तिमात्रेण प्राप्तितुष्टिर्मुहुर्मुहुः ॥ १०-४ ॥
bhavāsaṁsaktimātreṇa prāptituṣṭirmuhurmuhuḥ (10-4)

The very root of Bondage is cravings,
and the destruction of all cravings is Liberation.
By carefully cultivating utter indifference to all worldly things
—by becoming firmly rooted
in the seat of perfect dispassion—
one becomes established in pure bliss:
the Bliss of Realization.
So therefore always remain Equanimous.

त्वमेकश्चेतनः शुद्धो जडं विश्वमसत्तथा ।
tvamekaścetanaḥ śuddho jaḍaṁ viśvamasattathā ,
अविद्यापि न किञ्चित्सा का बुभुत्सा तथापि ते ॥ १०-५ ॥
avidyāpi na kiñcitsā kā bubhutsā tathāpi te (10-5)

You alone
—the One pristine Consciousness—
are Real and unfettered;
rest all is non-Real
—impermanent and bound into inertness.
Ignorance itself is nothing
—because it derives from the non-Real—
so what need have you of desiring to learn more and more?
Just abide in Equanimity.

राज्यं सुताः कलत्राणि शरीराणि सुखानि च ।
rājyaṁ sutāḥ kalatrāṇi śarīrāṇi sukhāni ca ,
संसक्तस्यापि नष्टानि तव जन्मनि जन्मनि ॥ १०-६ ॥
saṁsaktasyāpi naṣṭāni tava janmani janmani (10-6)

Over countless prior lives,
kingdoms, spouses, children, bodies, pleasures:
all these were gained
—but ultimately lost—
by you,
even though life after life
—just as now—
you were ever so lovingly attached to them.
You lost them then,
and you will lose them now
—so of what avail are these worldly things
which you so desperately cling to?
Why not just abide Equanimous?

अलमर्थेन कामेन सुकृतेनापि कर्मणा ।
alamarthena kāmena sukṛtenāpi karmaṇā ,
एभ्यः संसारकान्तारे न विश्रान्तमभून् मनः ॥ १०-७ ॥
ebhyaḥ saṁsārakāntāre na viśrāntamabhūn manaḥ (10-7)

Enough of sensuality,
enough of thirst for wealth,
enough even of pious deeds—
enough already!
In the dismal wilderness of the world,
who has ever found abiding repose in any of those?
Who? When? For how long?
Just think!
Just abide in Equanimity.

कृतं न कति जन्मानि कायेन मनसा गिरा ।
kṛtaṁ na kati janmāni kāyena manasā girā ,
दुःखमायासदं कर्म तदद्याप्युपरम्यताम् ॥ १०-८॥
duḥkhamāyāsadaṁ karma tadadyāpyuparamyatām (10-8)

In how many unnumbered births
have you not suffered harsh painful labor
of the body, mind, speech?
Desist even now.
In this life at least
just cease it all
—and come by peace!
Abide Equanimous.

:: End Canto – X ::

:: Canto – XI ::
- Wisdom -

अष्टावक्र उवाच

aṣṭāvakra uvāca:

भावाभावविकारश्च स्वभावादिति निश्चयी ।
bhāvābhāvavikāraśca svabhāvāditi niścayī ,
निर्विकारो गतक्लेशः सुखेनैवोपशाम्यति ॥ ११-१ ॥
nirvikāro gatakleśaḥ sukhenaivopaśāmyati (11-1)

Ashtāvakra said:
Ever changing appearances,
transmutation of names and forms—
and then an ultimate destruction of things
—that is Nature,
the very characteristics of the world of manifested existence.
Realizing this world to be ephemeral,
one comes by peace with ease
...remaining unperturbed undistressed unmoved.

ईश्वरः सर्वनिर्माता नेहान्य इति निश्चयी ।
īśvaraḥ sarvanirmātā nehānya iti niścayī ,
अन्तर्गलितसर्वाशः शान्तः क्वापि न सज्जते ॥ ११-२ ॥
antargalitasarvāśaḥ śāntaḥ kvāpi na sajjate (11-2)

With firm conviction having known of the *Ishwara*
—the Param-Ātmā-Rāma, the creator and source of the universe, the author of it all—
and having directly realized Him,
all hopes and wants for the world melt away;
and then remaining detached from everything extraneous,
one abides in peace.

आपदः सम्पदः काले दैवादेवेति निश्चयी ।
āpadaḥ sampadaḥ kāle daivādeveti niścayī ,
तृप्तः स्वस्थेन्द्रियो नित्यं न वान्छति न शोचति ॥ ११-३ ॥
tṛptaḥ svasthendriyo nityaṁ na vānchati na śocati (11-3)

At their decreed time,
misfortunes and fortunes will arrive by destiny's accord—
the inevitable result of one's own past karmas.
He who realizes this in full certainty,
freed of all doubts
he neither hopes nor laments nor is pained;
instead
with all his senses under control,
he abides ever content.

सुखदुःखे जन्ममृत्यू दैवादेवेति निश्चयी ।
sukhaduḥkhe janmamṛtyū daivādeveti niścayī ,
साध्यादर्शी निरायासः कुर्वन्नपि न लिप्यते ॥ ११-४ ॥
sādhyādarśī nirāyāsaḥ kurvannapi na lipyate (11-4)

Pleasures and sorrows, birth and death
are bestowed by destiny
and always come at their appointed time
—impelled by karmas from this life and prior.
Knowing this and certain in the knowledge
that no wishes can be attained unless karma has so ordained,
one remains tranquil;
and even though performing work intently,
one does not become attached
or ensnared any further.

चिन्तया जायते दुःखं नान्यथेहेति निश्चयी ।
cintayā jāyate duḥkhaṁ nānyatheheti niścayī ,
तया हीनः सुखी शान्तः सर्वत्र गलितस्पृहः ॥ ११-५ ॥
tayā hīnaḥ sukhī śāntaḥ sarvatra galitaspṛhaḥ (11-5)

Anxiety only produces misery and nothing else
—he who realizes this fully,
he rids himself of all anxiousness;
and thereafter abides he peaceful and happy,
thoroughly bereft of cravings and fancies.

नाहं देहो न मे देहो बोधोऽहमिति निश्चयी ।
nāhaṁ deho na me deho bodho'hamiti niścayī ,
कैवल्यं इव संप्राप्तो न स्मरत्यकृतं कृतम् ॥ ११-६ ॥
kaivalyam iva saṁprāpto na smaratyakṛtaṁ kṛtam (11-6)

"I am not the body
—nor is the body mine—
I am only a pure awareness,"
—having realized this directly,
one attains the state of
Onlyness.
Then to him everything appears dream-like;
and what he has done,
and what he has not done
—he can barely fathom at all.

आब्रह्मस्तम्बपर्यन्तं अहमेवेति निश्चयी ।
ābrahmastambaparyantaṁ ahameveti niścayī ,
निर्विकल्पः शुचिः शान्तः प्राप्ताप्राप्तविनिर्वृतः ॥ ११-७ ॥
nirvikalpaḥ śuciḥ śāntaḥ prāptāprāptavinirvṛtaḥ (11-7)

"Verily all this
—from Brahammā down to tiny bits of grass—
is just my own Self"
—having realized this with full certainty,
there is no more dubiety or conflicting thought;
and then the sage abides serene and pure,
no longer concerned with what may have been attained,
or what still remains unattained.

नाश्चर्यमिदं विश्वं न किञ्चिदिति निश्चयी ।
nāścaryamidaṁ viśvaṁ na kiñciditi niścayī ,
निर्वासनः स्फूर्तिमात्रो न किञ्चिदिव शाम्यति ॥ ११-८ ॥
nirvāsanaḥ sphūrtimātro na kiñcidiva śāmyati (11-8)

Having realized with complete certitude
that this seeming varicolored multifarious universe
—full of wonders, and elusive and delusive as magician's show—
is unreal and has been spun out of the Supreme-Self
to sparkle and show for just a little while,
—one rises above hankerings
and finds abiding peace within the Self
—to the exclusion of everything else—
...as if nothing else exists.

:: End Canto – XI ::

:: Canto – XII ::
- Onlyness -

जनक उवाच
janaka uvāca:

कायकृत्यासहः पूर्वं ततो वाग्विस्तरासहः ।
kāyakṛtyāsahaḥ pūrvaṁ tato vāgvistarāsahaḥ ,
अथ चिन्तासहस्तस्माद् एवमेवाहमास्थितः ॥ १२-१ ॥
atha cintāsahastasmād evamevāhamāsthitaḥ (12-1)

Janaka said:
At first I become averse to the actions of the body,
and then to prolonged speech;
and finally giving up even thinking itself—
that is how I now stand established
—completely unconcerned
...dwelling just within the sanctuary of The-One
...in Onlyness.

प्रीत्यभावेन शब्दादेरदृश्यत्वेन चात्मनः ।
prītyabhāvena śabdāderadṛśyatvena cātmanaḥ ,
विक्षेपैकाग्रहृदय एवमेवाहमास्थितः ॥ १२-२ ॥
vikṣepaikāgrahṛdaya evamevāhamāsthitaḥ (12-2)

Indifferent to delightful objects of sight and sound,
and unbothered even of my own self
—which is anyhow beyond perceptions and conceptions—
is how I now dwell:
completely untroubled,
freed of agitations and distractions,
taking recourse just in the
Onlyness of the Self.

समाध्यासादिविक्षिप्तौ व्यवहारः समाधये ।
samādhyāsādivikṣiptau vyavahāraḥ samādhaye ,
एवं विलोक्य नियममेवमेवाहमास्थितः ॥ १२-३ ॥
evaṁ vilokya niyamamevamevāhamāsthitaḥ (12-3)

It is only when there are distractions caused by superimpositions etc.,
that one makes efforts to be absorbed in Samadhi.
Seeing this to be the rule ...and so remaining completely uninvolved with the motley bag of superimpositions
—like body, ego, mind etc.—
I abide just within the sanctuary of the Ātmā
...in Onlyness.

हेयोपादेयविरहाद् एवं हर्षविषादयोः ।
heyopādeyavirahād evaṁ harṣaviṣādayoḥ ,
अभावादद्य हे ब्रह्मन्न् एवमेवाहमास्थितः ॥ १२-४ ॥
abhāvādadya he brahmann evamevāhamāsthitaḥ (12-4)

Having nothing to accept and nothing to reject;
admitting neither of sorrows nor joys
...to eschew or partake
—that is how, O master,
I abide in my present state
...in unwavering steadiness
...in the Ātmā's Onlyness.

आश्रमानाश्रमं ध्यानं चित्तस्वीकृतवर्जनम् ।
āśramānāśramaṁ dhyānaṁ cittasvīkṛtavarjanam ,
विकल्पं मम वीक्ष्यैतैरेवमेवाहमास्थितः ॥ १२-५ ॥
vikalpaṁ mama vīkṣyaitairevamevāhamāsthitaḥ (12-5)

Which way-of-life (āshrama) to adopt?
...or perhaps none at all?
which meditation to practice?
...and how?
the controlling of mind functions, etc., etc., ...so many divergent considerations—
all these are but distractions imposed upon the ever-free Ātmā.
Knowing of that
—and eliminating all such distracting vexations—
that is how I now abide
—steadfast in my Onlyness.

कर्मानुष्ठानमज्ञानाद् यथैवोपरमस्तथा ।
karmānuṣṭhānamajñānād yathaivoparamastathā ,
बुध्वा सम्यगिदं तत्त्वमेवमेवाहमास्थितः ॥ १२-६ ॥
budhvā samyagidaṁ tattvamevamevāhamāsthitaḥ (12-6)

Performance of karma
—impelled by wish to gain desired objectives of the world;
and also abandonment of karma
—born of fear, anxiety, sloth—
they are both indicative of
Nescience and Ignorance
—the enemies of Realization;
so fully compliant of this truth,
is how I now abide
—in the Onlyness of the Ātmā.

अचिन्त्यं चिन्त्यमानोऽपि चिन्तारूपं भजत्यसौ ।
acintyaṁ cintyamāno'pi cintārūpaṁ bhajatyasau ,
त्यक्त्वा तद्भावनं तस्माद् एवमेवाहमास्थितः ॥ १२-७ ॥
tyaktvā tadbhāvanaṁ tasmād evamevāhamāsthitaḥ (12-7)

To think upon the Unthinkable-One
—who is beyond the range of thought—
...is in itself a distraction in the form of an imposed thought—
an unneeded impediment.
Therefore giving up even such *sāttvika* thoughts,
is how I now stand established:
in the complete quietude of Ātmā's Onlyness.

एवमेव कृतं येन स कृतार्थो भवेदसौ ।
evameva kṛtaṁ yena sa kṛtārtho bhavedasau ,
एवमेव स्वभावो यः स कृतार्थो भवेदसौ ॥ १२-८ ॥
evameva svabhāvo yaḥ sa kṛtārtho bhavedasau (12-8)

He who abides entrenched in such
unwavering beatitude
—in the Onlyness of the Ātmā—
that soul is indeed blessed-most
—for he has achieved the purpose of human life:
having realized his Oneness in Brahama-Rāma.

:: End Canto – XII ::

:: Canto – XIII ::
- Felicity -

जनक उवाच
janaka uvāca:

अकिञ्चनभवं स्वास्थं कौपीनत्वेऽपि दुर्लभम् ।
akiñcanabhavaṁ svāsthaṁ kaupīnatve'pi durlabham ,
त्यागादाने विहायास्मादहमासे यथासुखम् ॥ १३-१ ॥
tyāgādāne vihāyāsmādahamāse yathāsukham (13-1)

Janaka said:
That quietude
—which is born of understanding that there just is the Self and nothing else—
—that inner freedom which springs from
'there's-nothing-else' to possess, or cope, or confront, or contend with—
—that is priceless.
That tranquility is hard to attain
—even by staunch renouncers who live wearing just a loin-cloth—
without the accompanying requisite: Self-Knowledge.
So, under all circumstances,
I abide only in Self-Knowledge—
abandoning both acquisition and renunciation.

कुत्रापि खेदः कायस्य जिह्वा कुत्रापि खेद्यते ।
kutrāpi khedaḥ kāyasya jihvā kutrāpi khedyate ,
मनः कुत्रापि तत्त्यक्त्वा पुरुषार्थे स्थितः सुखम् ॥ १३-२ ॥
manaḥ kutrāpi tattyaktvā puruṣārthe sthitaḥ sukham (13-2)

There is this hassle of the body here,
the troubles of the tongue there,
and the worries of the mind elsewhere;
knowing of these pitfalls
—and thus having renounced them all—
and rising above the unrests of the body
...and the tempestuousness of the senses
...and the cravings of the mind

—I abide just in the Bliss of the Ātmā
...which is the ultimate gain of one's existence.

कृतं किमपि नैव स्याद् इति सञ्चिन्त्य तत्त्वतः ।
kṛtaṁ kimapi naiva syād iti sañcintya tattvataḥ ,
यदा यत्कर्तुमायाति तत् कृत्वासे यथासुखम् ॥ १३-३ ॥
yadā yatkartumāyāti tat kṛtvāse yathāsukham (13-3)

"Nothing whatsoever is really done by the Self,
because the Ātmā is never a doer or agent,"
—fully realizing this truth,
I do only whatever presents itself before me
begging to be performed;
and this way,
free of commitments,
I only dwell in the Bliss of the Ātmā.

कर्मनैष्कर्म्यनिर्बन्धभावा देहस्थयोगिनः ।
karmanaiṣkarmyanirbandhabhāvā dehasthayoginaḥ ,
संयोगायोगविरहादहमासे यथासुखम् ॥ १३-४ ॥
saṁyogāyogavirahādahamāse yathāsukham (13-4)

Notions of Actions and Inaction are relevant
only for those attached to the body.
As for me,
having neither association nor dissociation with the body, ego, mind,
I abide only in the ceaseless Bliss of the Ātmā.

अर्थानर्थौ न मे स्थित्या गत्या न शयनेन वा ।
arthānarthau na me sthityā gatyā na śayanena vā ,
तिष्ठन् गच्छन् स्वपन् तस्मादहमासे यथासुखम् ॥ १३-५ ॥
tiṣṭhan gacchan svapan tasmādahamāse yathāsukham (13-5)

"Whether I am coming or going, active or inert,
it is no loss or gain for me
—of no pertinence whatsoever to me—
who am just an awareness pure, bereft of body,"
—with this attitude I now abide ever happy,
whether standing, sitting, walking, sleeping.

स्वपतो नास्ति मे हानिः सिद्धिर्यत्नवतो न वा ।
svapato nāsti me hāniḥ siddhiryatnavato na vā ,
नाशोल्लासौ विहायास्मदहमासे यथासुखम् ॥ १३-६ ॥
nāśollāsau vihāyāsmadahamāse yathāsukham (13-6)

Whether the body stays awake or asleep—
I neither lose nor gain this way or that.
Giving up all thoughts of sufferings and triumphs
—which are germane to the world and not to the Ātmā
—happily I abide.

सुखादिरूपा नियमं भावेष्वालोक्य भूरिशः ।
sukhādirūpā niyamaṁ bhāveṣvālokya bhūriśaḥ ,
शुभाशुभे विहायास्मादहमासे यथासुखम् ॥ १३-७ ॥
śubhāśubhe vihāyāsmādahamāse yathāsukham (13-7)

This motley bag of worldly joys and sorrows
is ever heavy but never constant
—changeful within the blink of an eye.
Thus,
having again and again observed the futility and fickleness inherent in
pursuits, pleasures, delights, hurts, sorrows
I have disowned the entire throng of dualities
—which are like piercing thorns—
and now I abide in a happy place
—in the Onlyness of the Ātmā pure.

:: End Canto – XIII ::

:: Canto – XIV ::
- Tranquility -

जनक उवाच
janaka uvāca:

प्रकृत्या शून्यचित्तो यः प्रमादाद् भावभावनः ।
prakṛtyā śūnyacitto yaḥ pramādād bhāvabhāvanaḥ ,
निद्रितो बोधित इव क्षीणसंस्मरणो हि सः ॥ १४-१ ॥
nidrito bodhita iva kṣīṇasaṁsmaraṇo hi saḥ (14-1)

Janaka said:
He, whose natural state of the mind is marked with vacuity
—who happens to think of things only mayhap—
who seems to be awake
...although really in a dream
—only that sage can be said to have expunged all impressions and experiences of the worldly life from within him.

क्व धनानि क्व मित्राणि क्व मे विषयदस्यवः ।
kva dhanāni kva mitrāṇi kva me viṣayadasyavaḥ ,
क्व शास्त्रं क्व च विज्ञानं यदा मे गलिता स्पृहा ॥ १४-२ ॥
kva śāstraṁ kva ca vijñānaṁ yadā me galitā spṛhā (14-2)

When all desires
have all melted away from the heart,
then,
...where exists any notion of wealth for me?
...where my friends and companions?
...where the sense-objects that rob one's peace of mind?
...where the weighty scriptures?
...and where the science of wisdom?

O thee Tranquility,
with my desires dissolved,
they too have all vanished as well;
and now I just have thee: O Tranquility.

विज्ञाते साक्षिपुरुषे परमात्मनि चेश्वरे ।
vijñāte sākṣipuruṣe paramātmani ceśvare ,
नैराश्ये बन्धमोक्षे च न चिन्ता मुक्तये मम ॥ १४-३ ॥
nairāśye bandhamokṣe ca na cintā muktaye mama (14-3)

Having realized
the Ātmā to be one in the Param-Ātmā
—the great Lord and the Witness of all—
I have become indifferent to the ideas of bondages and freedom.
I just abide Tranquil,
and I feel no anxiety even for emancipation.

अन्तर्विकल्पशून्यस्य बहिः स्वच्छन्दचारिणः ।
antarvikalpaśūnyasya bahiḥ svacchandacāriṇaḥ ,
भ्रान्तस्येव दशास्तास्तास्तादृशा एव जानते ॥ १४-४ ॥
bhrāntasyeva daśāstāstāstādṛśā eva jānate (14-4)

One who has become fully Realized,
free of illusions, freed of doubts,
might appear outwardly
to be like those still living in Ignorance,
...but that's not so really.
It takes one to know one;
verily the tranquil state of consciousness
of that exalted sage
is known only to another one like him.

:: End Canto – XIV ::

:: Canto – XV ::
- Essence of the Science of Self-Knowledge -

अष्टावक्र उवाच
aṣṭāvakra uvāca:

यथातथोपदेशेन कृतार्थः सत्त्वबुद्धिमान् ।
yathātathopadeśena kṛtārthaḥ sattvabuddhimān ,
आजीवमपि जिज्ञासुः परस्तत्र विमुह्यति ॥ १५-१ ॥
ājīvamapi jijñāsuḥ parastatra vimuhyati (15-1)

Ashtāvakra said:
A man of pure sāttvika mind,
realizes the Self even through instructions casually imparted;
but a man of muddied intellect
—whose mind is filled with the worldly-clutter—
persists bewildered;
and he may study all he wants
and enquire all throughout his life,
but remains he completely clueless.

मोक्षो विषयवैरस्यं बन्धो वैषयिको रसः ।
mokṣo viṣayavairasyaṁ bandho vaiṣayiko rasaḥ ,
एतावदेव विज्ञानं यथेच्छसि तथा कुरु ॥ १५-२ ॥
etāvadeva vijñānaṁ yathecchasi tathā kuru (15-2)

"A taste for sense-objects breeds Bondages;
and distaste for sense-objects begets Liberation,"
—this is the science of Self-Knowledge
put very succinctly;
and now act as thou wilt.

वाग्मिप्राज्ञामहोद्योगं जनं मूकजडालसम् ।
vāgmiprājñāmahodyogaṁ janaṁ mūkajaḍālasam ,
करोति तत्त्वबोधोऽयमतस्त्यक्तो बुभुक्षभिः ॥ १५-३ ॥
karoti tattvabodho'yamatastyakto bubhukṣabhiḥ (15-3)

The knowledge of the Ātmā and the Param-Ātmā
—the imperishable essence behind all existence—
transforms a hard-working eloquent intelligent man

to become unhurried, aloof, silent, dumb
—at least as seen from the outside.
The worldly crowd looks at this metamorphosis to be such a "sorry loss!",
and it is no wonder then,
that this Self-Knowledge is shunned by the stupe
who are so attached to the pleasures of the senses
...and nor it is really meant for those dunce.

न त्वं देहो न ते देहो भोक्ता कर्ता न वा भवान् ।
na tvaṁ deho na te deho bhoktā kartā na vā bhavān ,
चिद्रूपोऽसि सदा साक्षी निरपेक्षः सुखं चर ॥ १५-४ ॥
cidrūpo'si sadā sākṣī nirapekṣaḥ sukhaṁ cara (15-4)

You are not the body,
nor is the body yours;
you are not the doer of any action,
nor the partaker of the fruits of actions.
You are simply an awareness
—ever free, ever a silent witness.
First know of this supreme-science,
then go about happily through life.

रागद्वेषौ मनोधर्मौ न मनस्ते कदाचन ।
rāgadveṣau manodharmau na manaste kadācana ,
निर्विकल्पोऽसि बोधात्मा निर्विकारः सुखं चर ॥ १५-५ ॥
nirvikalpo'si bodhātmā nirvikāraḥ sukhaṁ cara (15-5)

Desire and aversion are attributes of the mind
—that state of consciousness which is
ever changing, ever scheming, ever in conflict.
Know that this mind is not you, or yours
—it never was, never will be.
You are far, far higher to the mind
—because you are the Ātmā:
pristine consciousness, immutable, free of conflict.
Embrace this supreme-science and dwell in bliss.

सर्वभूतेषु चात्मानं सर्वभूतानि चात्मनि ।
sarvabhūteṣu cātmānaṁ sarvabhūtāni cātmani ,
विज्ञाय निरहङ्कारो निर्ममस्त्वं सुखी भव ॥ १५-६ ॥
vijñāya nirahaṅkāro nirmamastvaṁ sukhī bhava (15-6)

"Realize that your Self is the Self of all
(and that all beings abide in that Supreme-Self);
and become bereft of the egoity of individuality
(be released of the sense of 'me' and 'mine');
and directly realize that you not the Jīva
but the Ātmā free of attributes,"
—this is the supreme-science of the Self
which leads one to the realm of endless Bliss.

विश्वं स्फुरति यत्रेदं तरङ्गा इव सागरे ।
viśvaṁ sphurati yatredaṁ taraṅgā iva sāgare ,
तत्त्वमेव न सन्देहश्चिन्मूर्ते विज्वरो भव ॥ १५-७ ॥
tattvameva na sandehaścinmūrte vijvaro bhava (15-7)

Thou art That Ocean of Consciousness
from which this universe has effloresced
—and which universe is now undulating like waves in that Ocean.
Freed of the febrility of the mind,
released of all doubts and agitations—
may thou abide in your innate essence:
as pristine Bliss and Consciousness.

श्रद्धस्व तात श्रद्धस्व नात्र मोऽहं कुरुष्व भोः ।
śraddhasva tāta śraddhasva nātra mo'haṁ kuruṣva bhoḥ ,
ज्ञानस्वरूपो भगवानात्मा त्वं प्रकृतेः परः ॥ १५-८ ॥
jñānasvarūpo bhagavānātmā tvaṁ prakṛteḥ paraḥ (15-8)

Have faith, O son, have faith!
Do not despair.
Know for sure:
You yourself are the Supreme-One,
the Knowledge Absolute,
the Sovereign Existence

—beyond nature, beyond the bounds of causation, beyond all laws.
Never again identify yourself
with any of these superimpositions.

गुणैः संवेष्टितो देहस्तिष्ठत्यायाति याति च ।
guṇaiḥ saṁveṣṭito dehastiṣṭhatyāyāti yāti ca ,
आत्मा न गन्ता नागन्ता किमेनमनुशोचसि ॥ १५-९ ॥
ātmā na gantā nāgantā kimenamanuśocasi (15-9)

This body,
invested with the *guna*s (attributes),
may be seen coming and going in the world
—kicking and screaming at birth
...or one day resting hushed in death—
but you yourself
—the Ātmā, the Self—
neither comes into existence
nor goes anywhere.
So why bother with any of these frolickings of life?
...wherefore celebrate, mourn, revel, grieve?
...for whom? ...and for what reason?

देहस्तिष्ठतु कल्पान्तं गच्छत्वद्यैव वा पुनः ।
dehastiṣṭhatu kalpāntaṁ gacchatvadyaiva vā punaḥ ,
क्व वृद्धिः क्व च वा हानिस्तव चिन्मात्ररूपिणः ॥ १५-१० ॥
kva vṛddhiḥ kva ca vā hānistava cinmātrarūpiṇaḥ (15-10)

Let this body last till the end of the world-cycle
...or let it fall away even today
—what matters that?
Nothing was bestowed
on the all-complete Ātmā
when the body became conjoined to It upon birth.
What will be reduced from that everlastingly perfect Ātmā
when the body drops away from It at death?
Nothing can be added or subtracted
from the Ātmā
—which is pure awareness.

त्वय्यनन्तमहाम्भोधौ विश्ववीचिः स्वभावतः ।
tvayyanantamahāmbhodhau viśvavīciḥ svabhāvataḥ ,
उदेतु वास्तमायातु न ते वृद्धिर्न वा क्षतिः ॥१५-११॥
udetu vāstamāyātu na te vṛddhirna vā kṣatiḥ (15-11)

In the infinite Ocean which is thee,
the waves of the universe go up and down
like drifting rolling flourishes,
each following its innate trait.
Let them rise
let them fall,
they do not touch thee at all.

तात चिन्मात्ररूपोऽसि न ते भिन्नमिदं जगत् ।
tāta cinmātrarūpo'si na te bhinnamidaṁ jagat ,
अतः कस्य कथं कुत्र हेयोपादेयकल्पना ॥१५-१२॥
ataḥ kasya kathaṁ kutra heyopādeyakalpanā (15-12)

My child,
your essence is pure Consciousness
—pristine and unsullied at the core.
And the perception you have of the universe
is indeed only within that awareness
[which has albeit become sullied and muddied and no longer abides pristine—with the taint of the universe having become seen in it].
Being that the universe thus seen
is indeed indistinct from your awareness,
and cannot become separated from it,
so then,
the thought of rejecting or accepting anything
is quite meaningless really.

Within a Oneness,
who's there to reject or accept what?
...and how ...and why?

एकस्मिन्नव्यये शान्ते चिदाकाशेऽमले त्वयि ।
ekasminnavyaye śānte cidākāśe'male tvayi ,
कुतो जन्म कुतो कर्म कुतोऽहङ्कार एव च ॥ १५-१३ ॥
kuto janma kuto karma kuto'haṅkāra eva ca (15-13)

You are the eternal one, pristine consciousness
—immutable, tranquil, taintless.
For you, how can there be any birth and body?
or duties, works, doings?
or even egoism and a mind?
...being that that would be at odds
with your origin and essence.

यत्त्वं पश्यसि तत्रैकस्त्वमेव प्रतिभाससे ।
yattvaṁ paśyasi tatraikastvameva pratibhāsase ,
किं पृथक् भासते स्वर्णात् कटकाङ्गदनूपुरम् ॥ १५-१४ ॥
kiṁ pṛthak bhāsate svarṇāt kaṭakāṅgadanūpuram (15-14)

In whatever is seen manifested here
—it is you yourSelf who appears.
Are the jewelries forged from gold
—like bracelets, armlets, rings etc., —
anything at all different
from the gold of which they are made?

अयं सोऽहमयं नाहं विभागमिति सन्त्यज ।
ayaṁ so'hamayaṁ nāhaṁ vibhāgamiti santyaja ,
सर्वमात्मेति निश्चित्य निःसङ्कल्पः सुखी भव ॥ १५-१५ ॥
sarvamātmeti niścitya niḥsaṅkalpaḥ sukhī bhava (15-15)

Renouncing all notions of 'such' and 'so',
effacing all distinctions such as
'I am this here', 'and not that',
know everything here to be just your own Self;
and thus freed of all cravings for an 'other',
abide ever content.

तवैवाज्ञानतो विश्वं त्वमेकः परमार्थतः ।
tavaivājñānato viśvaṁ tvamekaḥ paramārthataḥ ,
त्वत्तोऽन्यो नास्ति संसारी नासंसारी च कश्चन ॥ १५-१६ ॥
tvatto'nyo nāsti saṁsārī nāsaṁsārī ca kaścana (15-16)

The universe is the outcome of Nescience
—Ignorance of your Self.
Actually you alone exist,
there being nothing else.
In reality,
there is neither the Jīva (the bound soul)
nor the Īshwara (the Lord-God)
—existing as two distinct entities.
Aye, there is nothing whatsoever in existence
other than the One Param-Ātmā-Rāma.

भ्रान्तिमात्रमिदं विश्वं न किञ्चिदिति निश्चयी ।
bhrāntimātramidaṁ viśvaṁ na kiñciditi niścayī ,
निर्वासनः स्फूर्तिमात्रो न किञ्चिदिव शाम्यति ॥ १५-१७ ॥
nirvāsanaḥ sphūrtimātro na kiñcidiva śāmyati (15-17)

One who fully realizes
that the manifest universe is purely a conjuration,
an illusion,
a deluding dance of Rāma's Māyā
—a play enacted by Brahama Rāma, the Supreme-Self, with a view to sport—
he becomes desireless,
[...because what sane person would desire to reach out for a non-Real mirage?]
and he comes by everlasting peace
—having become one with the only existent Reality—
...there being nothing else.

एक एव भवाम्भोधावासीदस्ति भविष्यति ।
eka eva bhavāmbhodhāvāsīdasti bhaviṣyati ,
न ते बन्धोऽस्ति मोक्षो वा कृत्यकृत्यः सुखं चर ॥ १५-१८॥
na te bandho'sti mokṣo vā kṛtyakṛtyaḥ sukhaṁ cara (15-18)

In this worldly ocean,
there is just a One-Consciousness in Existence
—was, is, will be.
In reality, you have neither any bondages
nor a need for freedom
—because you already abide Independent.
Possessed of this knowledge
—and living in accordance with that—
be happy.

मा सङ्कल्पविकल्पाभ्यां चित्तं क्षोभय चिन्मय ।
mā saṅkalpavikalpābhyāṁ cittaṁ kṣobhaya cinmaya ,
उपशाम्य सुखं तिष्ठ स्वात्मन्यानन्दविग्रहे ॥ १५-१९॥
upaśāmya sukhaṁ tiṣṭha svātmanyānandavigrahe (15-19)

Why are you
—who are just a pristine awareness—
bothered with extraneous considerations?
Why stress yourself with notions such as: towards, against,
avowal, disavowal, acquiring, relinquishing, this, that?
Simply be calm and abide happy as your own Self,
in your innate essence
—which is Bliss itself.

त्यजैव ध्यानं सर्वत्र मा किञ्चिद् हृदि धारय ।
tyajaiva dhyānaṁ sarvatra mā kiñcid hṛdi dhāraya ,
आत्मा त्वं मुक्त एवासि किं विमृश्य करिष्यसि ॥ १५-२०॥
ātmā tvaṁ mukta evāsi kiṁ vimṛśya kariṣyasi (15-20)

Simply be your Self: the Ātmā,
relinquishing all taints on that pristine awareness.
Hold to no thoughts within
—even the thought of meditation.
You are free already,
so why aspire for liberation?
Why search for joy—you yourself are happiness.
What will you accomplish by any thought?
—which is just a taint
on the spotlessness of your Self.

:: End Canto – XV ::

:: Canto – XVI ::
- Special Instruction -

अष्टावक्र उवाच
aṣṭāvakra uvāca:

आचक्ष्व शृणु वा तात नानाशास्त्राण्यनेकशः ।
ācakṣva śṛṇu vā tāta nānāśāstrāṇyanekaśaḥ ,
तथापि न तव स्वास्थ्यं सर्वविस्मरणाद् ऋते ॥ १६-१ ॥
tathāpi na tava svāsthyaṁ sarvavismaraṇād ṛte (16-1)

Ashtāvakra said:
My son;
you may listen, recite, debate all you want
and study countless scriptures,
but you will not get established in your innate essence
—that of being the blissful Ātmā, spotless, bereft of the taints of perceptions, knowledge, thoughts etc.,—
until, forgetting it all,
you actually step across the threshold—
directly into the realm of pristine non-duality.

भोगं कर्म समाधिं वा कुरु विज्ञ तथापि ते ।
bhogaṁ karma samādhiṁ vā kuru vijña tathāpi te ,
चित्तं निरस्तसर्वाशमत्यर्थं रोचयिष्यति ॥ १६-२ ॥
cittaṁ nirastasarvāśamatyarthaṁ rocayiṣyati (16-2)

O wise soul!
You may take delight all you want
in pleasures, things, work, words, thoughts, contemplation etc.,
—but your heart will continue yearning for its innate essence,
for its origin, the source it came from
...the home it so yearns to return to.
Aye, you will not find true rest
until you rest in that realm which is beyond all objects,
where all desires naturally lie extinguished.

आयासात्सकलो दुःखी नैनं जानाति कश्चन ।
āyāsātsakalo duḥkhī nainaṁ jānāti kaścana ,
अनेनैवोपदेशेन धन्यः प्राप्नोति निर्वृतिम् ॥ १६-३ ॥
anenaivopadeśena dhanyaḥ prāpnoti nirvṛtim (16-3)

People are in misery on account of their own exertions—
it's a pain caused by their own travails
...self inflicted;
but alas, who really understands that?
But one who is fortunate enough to understand and act on it,
he forthwith attains emancipation.

व्यापारे खिद्यते यस्तु निमेषोन्मेषयोरपि ।
vyāpāre khidyate yastu nimeṣonmeṣayorapi ,
तस्यालस्य धुरीणस्य सुखं नन्यस्य कस्यचित् ॥ १६-४ ॥
tasyālasya dhurīṇasya sukhaṁ nanyasya kasyacit (16-4)

True Bliss
—bliss which never ends,
which emanates without a cause,
which springs without an external impetus,
which has no bearing to anything material—
only belongs to a leisured master
—a master to whom all extraneous efforts,
even the closing and opening of the eyelids
is a beleaguered affliction—
and to none else.

इदं कृतमिदं नेति द्वन्द्वैर्मुक्तं यदा मनः ।
idaṁ kṛtamidaṁ neti dvandvairmuktaṁ yadā manaḥ ,
धर्मार्थकाममोक्षेषु निरपेक्षं तदा भवेत् ॥ १६-५ ॥
dharmārthakāmamokṣeṣu nirapekṣaṁ tadā bhavet (16-5)

When the mind is freed of the interminable list of burdensome conflicts such as:
"this is a must-do" and "this is strictly no-no",
then it becomes indifferent to everything,
remaining totally unconcerned with regards to gaining or losing anything

—be it religious merits, or worldly prosperities or pleasures, and what have you...
...even freedom and emancipation.

विरक्तो विषयद्वेष्टा रागी विषयलोलुपः ।
virakto viṣayadveṣṭā rāgī viṣayalolupaḥ ,
ग्रहमोक्षविहीनस्तु न विरक्तो न रागवान् ॥ १६-६ ॥
grahamokṣavihīnastu na virakto na rāgavān (16-6)

He who loathes sense-objects
is in embrace of dispassionateness;
and he who covets them
is in embrace of passionateness.
In truth both become fettered
—by dint of their hate and love—
whereas a person
who neither accepts nor shuns
—who neither runs away nor runs towards
the world—
displays True Non-attachment,
which has its roots in Indifference and Aloofness.

हेयोपादेयता तावत्संसारविटपाङ्कुरः ।
heyopādeyatā tāvatsaṁsāraviṭapāṅkuraḥ ,
स्पृहा जीवति यावद् वै निर्विचारदशास्पदम् ॥ १६-७ ॥
spṛhā jīvati yāvad vai nirvicāradaśāspadam (16-7)

The notion of desire and aversion is born of Nescience
—which is the absence of discrimination between the Real and non-Real.
The tree of phenomenal-existence arises from this duality of attraction and repulsion.
As soon as the mind "draws-towards"
or "draws-away" from anything
—forthwith this whole world comes into sprout,
before erupting into rampant bloom.

प्रवृत्तौ जायते रागो निर्वृत्तौ द्वेष एव हि ।
pravṛttau jāyate rāgo nirvṛttau dveṣa eva hi ,
निर्द्वन्द्वो बालवद् धीमान् एवमेव व्यवस्थितः ॥ १६-८ ॥
nirdvandvo bālavad dhīmān evameva vyavasthitaḥ (16-8)

Activity generates desire
while renunciation engenders aversion.
But true freedom is in pristine innocence,
an indifference born from being completely immersed in the bliss of the Ātmā
—where worldly affairs appear like evanescent things of no significance.
The wise lives like an innocent child,
free of turmoils of the mind.

हातुमिच्छति संसारं रागी दुःखजिहासया ।
hātumicchati saṁsāraṁ rāgī duḥkhajihāsayā ,
वीतरागो हि निर्दुःखस्तस्मिन्नपि न खिद्यति ॥ १६-९ ॥
vītarāgo hi nirduḥkhastasminnapi na khidyati (16-9)

One who desires to renounce the world
in order to avoid suffering,
is still found attached to the world
[—fettered with the bonds of avoidance];
but the wise simply has no attachments
[—even the adhesion of shunning it from fear];
and he suffers no misery
....from this dream called life.

यस्याभिमानो मोक्षेऽपि देहेऽपि ममता तथा ।
yasyābhimāno mokṣe'pi dehe'pi mamatā tathā ,
न च ज्ञानी न वा योगी केवलं दुःखभागसौ ॥ १६-१० ॥
na ca jñānī na vā yogī kevalaṁ duḥkhabhāgasau (16-10)

He who yearns for emancipation
—but still considers this body to be 'mine'—
he is neither wise, nor a yogi;
and his only lot in life is suffering
—as long as he continues
to retain the egoistic impression of 'I'-ness.

हरो यद्युपदेष्टा ते हरिः कमलजोऽपि वा ।
haro yadyupadeṣṭā te hariḥ kamalajo'pi vā ,
तथापि न तव स्वाथ्यं सर्वविस्मरणादृते ॥ १६-११ ॥
tathāpi na tava svāthyaṁ sarvavismaraṇādṛte (16-11)

Even if gods Shiva, Vishnu and the lotus-born Brahammā
themselves were to instruct you,
you will not become established in your innate essence,
until you
—giving up the imaginations of the non-Real—
have let your individual-self
—the I—
submerge within the Supreme-Self.

:: End Canto – XVI ::

:: Canto – XVII ::
- The Self-Realized Sage -

अष्टावक्र उवाच
aṣṭāvakra uvāca:

तेन ज्ञानफलं प्राप्तं योगाभ्यासफलं तथा ।
tena jñānaphalaṁ prāptaṁ yogābhyāsaphalaṁ tathā ,
तृप्तः स्वच्छेन्द्रियो नित्यमेकाकी रमते तु यः ॥ १७-१ ॥
tṛptaḥ svacchendriyo nityamekākī ramate tu yaḥ (17-1)

Ashtāvakra said:
When one remains ever contented
—always detached, with senses purified,
taking delight only in solitude—
then know that the fruits of
the practice of Yoga and Knowledge
have been attained.

न कदाचिज्जगत्यस्मिन् तत्त्वज्ञो हन्त खिद्यति ।
na kadācijjagatyasmin tattvajño hanta khidyati ,
यत एकेन तेनेदं पूर्णं ब्रह्माण्डमण्डलम् ॥ १७-२ ॥
yata ekena tenedaṁ pūrṇaṁ brahmāṇḍamaṇḍalam (17-2)

The knower of Truth undergoes no sufferings
—either inwardly or outwardly—
for he knows that:
"the entire expanse of the universe
exists in me
and is occupied by just me."

न जातु विषयाः केऽपि स्वारामं हर्षयन्त्यमी ।
na jātu viṣayāḥ ke'pi svārāmaṁ harṣayantyamī ,
सल्लकीपल्लवप्रीतमिवेभं निम्बपल्लवाः ॥ १७-३ ॥
sallakīpallavaprītamivebhaṁ nimbapallavāḥ (17-3)

No sense-objects can please him
who revels just in the Param-Ātmā Rāma
—even as an elephant
who takes natural delight in partaking the leaves of *Sallaki* plant,
leaves the bitter leaves of *Nima* trees well alone,
not even coming near them.

यस्तु भोगेषु भुक्तेषु न भवत्यधिवासितः ।
yastu bhogeṣu bhukteṣu na bhavatyadhivāsitaḥ ,
अभुक्तेषु निराकाङ्क्षी तदृशो भवदुर्लभः ॥ १७-४ ॥
abhukteṣu nirākāṅkṣī tadṛśo bhavadurlabhaḥ (17-4)

He who never again craves
for what he has once partaken,
and who does not hanker
after that which he has never had
—rare indeed is such a soul
upon whom no impressions are left of things.

बुभुक्षुरिह संसारे मुमुक्षुरपि दृश्यते ।
bubhukṣuriha saṁsāre mumukṣurapi dṛśyate ,
भोगमोक्षनिराकाङ्क्षी विरलो हि महाशयः ॥ १७-५ ॥
bhogamokṣanirākāṅkṣī viralo hi mahāśayaḥ (17-5)

There are those who crave for the mundane pleasures of the world,
and there are those who yearn for the highest bliss born of *Moksha*,
but rare is that great soul who cares for neither:
neither for the worldly joys,
nor for the bliss of *Nirvāna*.

धर्मार्थकाममोक्षेषु जीविते मरणे तथा ।
dharmārthakāmamokṣeṣu jīvite maraṇe tathā ,
कस्याप्युदारचित्तस्य हेयोपादेयता न हि ॥ १७-६ ॥
kasyāpyudāracittasya heyopādeyatā na hi (17-6)

It's only a rare noble sage
who abides indifferent to all of the four endeavors seen
impelling humankind:
Dharma (duty/virtue), *Artha* (prosperity), *Kāma* (desires)—and
even *Moksha* (liberation).
He neither embraces them nor shuns them;
and he is aloof even if this body were to stay draped upon him,
or if it were to fall away even today.

वाञ्छा न विश्वविलये न द्वेषस्तस्य च स्थितौ ।
vāñchā na viśvavilaye na dveṣastasya ca sthitau ,
यथा जीविकया तस्माद् धन्य आस्ते यथा सुखम् ॥ १७-७॥
yathā jīvikayā tasmād dhanya āste yathā sukham (17-7)

The wise does not desire for the dissolution of the universe,
and he has no aversion if it continues in existence.
With his mind ever detached
that blessed one abides happy—
ever content with whatever sustenance comes his way
in the natural course of things.

कृतार्थोऽनेन ज्ञानेनेत्येवं गलितधीः कृती ।
kṛtārtho'nena jñānenetyevaṁ galitadhīḥ kṛtī ,
पश्यन् श्रृण्वन् स्पृशन् जिघ्रन्न् अश्नन्नास्ते यथा सुखम् ॥ १७-८॥
paśyan śṛṇvan spṛśan jighrann aśnannāste yathā sukham (17-8)

Complete in the realization of the Self,
with his mind dissolved
—and thus with everything achieved—
the sage lives contented and in a state of bliss,
unconcerned as to what was seen, heard, touched, smelled, or
partaken by his body.

शून्या दृष्टिर्वृथा चेष्टा विकलानीन्द्रियाणि च ।
śūnyā dṛṣṭirvṛthā ceṣṭā vikalānīndriyāṇi ca ,
न स्पृहा न विरक्तिर्वा क्षीणसंसारसागरे ॥ १७-९॥
na spṛhā na viraktirvā kṣīṇasaṁsārasāgare (17-9)

Attachment and detachment are of no concern to him for whom this world of manifestations has dried up.
He has a vacant look about him—
...his senses inoperative
...his actions motiveless
...his attention withdrawn into the within realm:
the realm of the Ātmā.

न जागर्ति न निद्राति नोन्मीलति न मीलति ।
na jāgarti na nidrāti nonmīlati na mīlati ,
अहो परदशा क्वापि वर्तते मुक्तचेतसः ॥ १७-१० ॥
aho paradaśā kvāpi vartate muktacetasaḥ (17-10)

Neither asleep nor awake,
his eyes not open or closed,
the liberated one
—who abides freed of the mind—
simply dwells in the supreme non-dual realm.
He revels in the bliss of the Ātmā under every circumstance.

सर्वत्र दृश्यते स्वस्थः सर्वत्र विमलाशयः ।
sarvatra dṛśyate svasthaḥ sarvatra vimalāśayaḥ ,
समस्तवासना मुक्तो मुक्तः सर्वत्र राजते ॥ १७-११ ॥
samastavāsanā mukto muktaḥ sarvatra rājate (17-11)

He who has become liberated,
remains ever-rooted to his own essence
—abiding within his own Self.
Free of the within desires,
free of inclinations,
detached under all conditions,
he dwells in pristine innocence,
ever shining in his wholesome pureness.

पश्यन् शृण्वन् स्पृशन् जिघ्रन्न् अश्नन् गृण्हन् वदन् व्रजन् ।
paśyan śṛṇvan spṛśan jighrann aśnan gṛṇhan vadan vrajan ,
ईहितानीहितैर्मुक्तो मुक्त एव महाशयः ॥ १७-१२ ॥
īhitānīhitairmukto mukta eva mahāśayaḥ (17-12)

Even though visibly engaged in the activities of seeing, hearing, touching, smelling, eating, taking, talking, walking, the exalted sage is still held to be emancipated
—for he has risen above the ideas of acquiring and avoiding, remaining free of all fetters associated with action and inaction.

न निन्दति न च स्तौति न हृष्यति न कुप्यति ।
na nindati na ca stauti na hṛṣyati na kupyati ,
न ददाति न गृण्हाति मुक्तः सर्वत्र नीरसः ॥१७-१३॥
na dadāti na gṛṇhāti muktaḥ sarvatra nīrasaḥ (17-13)

He who has become liberated
neither censures nor commends,
neither exuberates nor gets infuriated,
neither gives up nor takes.
He is simply aloof
—free of the idea of attachments—
either of the positive or the negative genre.

सानुरागां स्त्रियं दृष्ट्वा मृत्युं वा समुपस्थितम् ।
sānurāgāṁ striyaṁ dṛṣṭvā mṛtyuṁ vā samupasthitam ,
अविह्वलमनाः स्वस्थो मुक्त एव महाशयः ॥१७-१४॥
avihvalamanāḥ svastho mukta eva mahāśayaḥ (17-14)

That exalted sage is considered emancipated
who is ever equipoised
—who remains unruffled and unperturbed under every circumstance—
whether it's the alluring sight of a seductive woman come near,
or his own death confronting him face to face.

सुखे दुःखे नरे नार्यां सम्पत्सु च विपत्सु च ।
sukhe duḥkhe nare nāryāṁ sampatsu ca vipatsu ca ,
विशेषो नैव धीरस्य सर्वत्र समदर्शिनः ॥१७-१५॥
viśeṣo naiva dhīrasya sarvatra samadarśinaḥ (17-15)

The tranquil sage of perfect equanimity
perceives the exact same sameness everywhere;
he catches no difference between
pleasure and pain,
man and woman,
prosperity and adversity.

न हिंसा नैव कारुण्यं नौद्धत्यं न च दीनता ।
na hiṁsā naiva kāruṇyaṁ nauddhatyaṁ na ca dīnatā ,
नाश्चर्यं नैव च क्षोभः क्षीणसंसरणे नरे ॥ १७-१६ ॥
nāścaryaṁ naiva ca kṣobhaḥ kṣīṇasaṁsaraṇe nare (17-16)

For the wise
—who is no more ensnared in Ignorance,
and consequently whose worldly life has become extinguished thereby—
there is neither a wish to harm another,
nor the want to offer consolation to others;
he experiences neither humility nor insolence,
neither wonder nor unrest—
because his material life has become exhausted.

न मुक्तो विषयद्वेष्टा न वा विषयलोलुपः ।
na mukto viṣayadveṣṭā na vā viṣayalolupaḥ ,
असंसक्तमना नित्यं प्राप्ताप्राप्तमुपाश्नुते ॥ १७-१७ ॥
asaṁsaktamanā nityaṁ prāptāprāptamupāśnute (17-17)

The liberated one
neither abhors sense-objects,
nor craves after them.
Ever of detached attitude
—rising above the notions of
gain loss, accumulating dissipating—
he experiences life as it comes,
as and when things
choose to present themselves in their due course.

समाधानसमाधानहिताहितविकल्पनाः ।
samādhānasamādhānahitāhitavikalpanāḥ ,
शून्यचित्तो न जानाति कैवल्यमिव संस्थितः ॥ १७-१८॥
śūnyacitto na jānāti kaivalyamiva saṁsthitaḥ (17-18)

One who has reached the vacuity of nothingness
—whose mind has melted—
is unaware even of differences in conflicting states
—like harmony-disharmony, resolution-conflict,
good-bad etc.
Transcending all dualities,
he has stepped across the threshold of the world
—and reached the realm of the Absolute-Singularity.

निर्ममो निरहङ्कारो न किञ्चिदिति निश्चितः ।
nirmamo nirahaṅkāro na kiñciditi niścitaḥ ,
अन्तर्गलितसर्वाशः कुर्वन्नपि करोति न ॥ १७-१९॥
antargalitasarvāśaḥ kurvannapi karoti na (17-19)

With desires dissipated,
void of the feeling of 'I' and 'mine',
certain only in the knowledge that nothing objective exists in reality,
the knower of Truth dwells in abiding peace
within the Ātmā.
He performs no karmas whatsoever
—although appearing to be engaged in action.

मनःप्रकाशसंमोहस्वप्नजाड्यविवर्जितः ।
manaḥprakāśasaṁmohasvapnajāḍyavivarjitaḥ ,
दशां कामपि सम्प्राप्तो भवेद् गलितमानसः ॥ १७-२०॥
daśāṁ kāmapi samprāpto bhaved galitamānasaḥ (17-20)

Certainly that highest state is indescribable
which that sage eventually gets to experience,
when having gone beyond it all
—beyond delusion, action, inertness, wakefulness, dream,
deep sleep, everything—
...when he actually steps across into that vestal realm...
...where everything has dropped away
...where the mind lies completely dissolved
—its functions having ceased to operate.

:: End Canto – XVII ::

:: Canto – XVIII ::

- Serenity -

अष्टावक्र उवाच

aṣṭāvakra uvāca:

यस्य बोधोदये तावत्स्वप्नवद् भवति भ्रमः ।

yasya bodhodaye tāvatsvapnavad bhavati bhramaḥ ,

तस्मै सुखैकरूपाय नमः शान्ताय तेजसे ॥ १८-१ ॥

tasmai sukhaikarūpāya namaḥ śāntāya tejase (18-1)

Ashtāvakra said:

Salutation to that Fiery Light—
self-effulgent, self-existent, independent,
which is pristine consciousness
which is tranquility,
which is bliss,
which is abiding existence—
in whose dawn,
this dark delusive universe
—which has the world enslaved—
vanishes away
like the dream of a dark night.

अर्जयित्वाखिलान् अर्थान् भोगानाप्नोति पुष्कलान् ।

arjayitvākhilān arthān bhogānāpnoti puṣkalān ,

न हि सर्वपरित्यागमन्तरेण सुखी भवेत् ॥ १८-२ ॥

na hi sarvaparityāgamantareṇa sukhī bhavet (18-2)

One can get ephemeral enjoyments by acquiring assorted worldly things,
but true happiness comes
only when one has renounced everything.
All things of the world are attended with dependency and fear of loss;
renunciation alone eliminates every concern.

कर्तव्यदुःखमार्तण्डज्वालादग्धान्तरात्मनः ।
kartavyaduḥkhamārtaṇḍajvālādagdhāntarātmanaḥ ,
कुतः प्रशमपीयूषधारासारमृते सुखम् ॥ १८-३ ॥
kutaḥ praśamapīyūṣadhārāsāramṛte sukham (18-3)

The heart easily becomes parched
from the heat of scorching sun of afflictions
—in the form of must-do-duties—
and unless there were the accompanying continuous shower of ambrosia
—of the tranquility of the Ātmā—
could an iota of happiness have been possible in the world?
Aye, it's only from the fiery glow of the Ātmā
where even the worldly people get continually invigorated
—albeit indirectly.

भवोऽयं भावनामात्रो न किञ्चित् परमर्थतः ।
bhavo'yaṁ bhāvanāmātro na kiñcit paramarthataḥ ,
नास्त्यभावः स्वभावानां भावाभावविभाविनाम् ॥ १८-४ ॥
nāstyabhāvaḥ svabhāvānāṁ bhāvābhāvavibhāvinām (18-4)

This Universe is but a modified state of the Supreme-Consciousness
[—albeit a sullied spot upon Its natural pristine essence].
In reality the universe is nothing
[has no independent existence
—being but a blot upon the Consciousness
of the Abiding Unmanifest Reality].
Having discerned the manifest from the Unmanifest,
those who thereafter dwell completely identified with that Unmanifest-Reality alone,
they become Immortal.

न दूरं न च सङ्कोचाल्लब्धमेवात्मनः पदम् ।
na dūraṁ na ca saṅkocāllabdhamevātmanaḥ padam ,
निर्विकल्पं निरायासं निर्विकारं निरञ्जनम् ॥ १८-५ ॥
nirvikalpaṁ nirāyāsaṁ nirvikāraṁ nirañjanam (18-5)

The Param-Ātmā
—the Singularity of the Absolute—
is the only Reality which exists ...but which has no cause,
which is without an external support, without a recourse,
which is without a taint, without any possibility of change.
That Ātmā is not far removed—rather It is the nearest;
The Ātmā is not limited—but is infinite in space;
The Ātmā is not an aim of attainment
—rather is already attained:
being one's own Self.

व्यामोहमात्रविरतौ स्वरूपादानमात्रतः ।
vyāmohamātraviratau svarūpādānamātrataḥ ,
वीतशोका विराजन्ते निरावरणदृष्टयः ॥ १८-६ ॥
vītaśokā virājante nirāvaraṇadṛṣṭayaḥ (18-6)

With their delusions dispelled,
those who abide cognized of the Self
—the fiery glow of pure consciousness shining within—
their distress is now at end;
and they live free of sorrows
—in the completeness of everlasting Bliss.

समस्तं कल्पनामात्रमात्मा मुक्तः सनातनः ।
samastaṁ kalpanāmātramātmā muktaḥ sanātanaḥ ,
इति विज्ञाय धीरो हि किमभ्यस्यति बालवत् ॥ १८-७ ॥
iti vijñāya dhīro hi kimabhyasyati bālavat (18-7)

Knowing all this to be just a conception enacted in the
imagination of the One Supreme Consciousness,
and knowing himself to be one in that Param Ātmā
—eternal, infinite, unfettered—
will a wise person childishly indulge
in the activities and practices of the worldly kind?
...which would only further enhance Nescience?

आत्मा ब्रह्मेति निश्चित्य भावाभावौ च कल्पितौ ।
ātmā brahmeti niścitya bhāvābhāvau ca kalpitau ,
निष्कामः किं विजानाति किं ब्रूते च करोति किम् ॥ १८-८ ॥
niṣkāmaḥ kiṁ vijānāti kiṁ brūte ca karoti kim (18-8)

Having finally realized that the Jīva is the Ātmā,
and that the Ātmā is Brahama
—the Supreme Unmanifest—
and that all manifest existence is an imagination spun out from within that Unmanifest,
what further remains for the desireless sage
to learn, to say, to do
...in this phantasma like manifested dream called the universe?

अयं सोऽहमयं नाहमिति क्षीणा विकल्पना ।
ayaṁ so'hamayaṁ nāhamiti kṣīṇā vikalpanā ,
सर्वमात्मेति निश्चित्य तूष्णीम्भूतस्य योगिनः ॥ १८-९ ॥
sarvamātmeti niścitya tūṣṇīmbhūtasya yoginaḥ (18-9)

All imaginations such as
"this indeed I am" and "this I am not"
stand decimated for the yogi.
Having confirmed
—in direct Realization—
that everything is just the Ātmā,
he falls silent.

न विक्षेपो न चैकाग्र्यं नातिबोधो न मूढता ।
na vikṣepo na caikāgryaṁ nātibodho na mūḍhatā ,
न सुखं न च वा दुःखमुपशान्तस्य योगिनः ॥ १८-१० ॥
na sukhaṁ na ca vā duḥkhamupaśāntasya yoginaḥ (18-10)

For the yogi who has become Realized
—who now owns That-Innate-Bliss—
there is
no more trying to meditate or getting distracted,
no more enhancement of knowledge or suffering from its lack,
no more of the worldly joys or the lack-of-joys
—because there simply is no more dualities of any kind.

स्वाराज्ये भैक्षवृत्तौ च लाभालाभे जने वने ।
svārājye bhaikṣavṛttau ca lābhālābhe jane vane ,
निर्विकल्पस्वभावस्य न विशेषोऽस्ति योगिनः ॥ १८-११ ॥
nirvikalpasvabhāvasya na viśeṣo'sti yoginaḥ (18-11)

Whether holding the sovereignty of a kingdom
or living in mendicancy,
whether making gains or suffering losses,
whether dwelling amidst multitudes
or in arrant solitude—
none of that makes any difference to the yogi,
who abides mentally freed of all conditions.

क्व धर्मः क्व च वा कामः क्व चार्थः क्व विवेकिता ।
kva dharmaḥ kva ca vā kāmaḥ kva cārthaḥ kva vivekitā ,
इदं कृतमिदं नेति द्वन्द्वैर्मुक्तस्य योगिनः ॥ १८-१२ ॥
idaṁ kṛtamidaṁ neti dvandvairmuktasya yoginaḥ (18-12)

The yogi who abides transcending dualities
—who has risen above conflicts of instructions and prohibitions
like "this ought to be done", and "this ought not"
—for him,
where is *Dharma*?
where *Kāma*?
where *Artha*?
where *Viveka*?
Such endeavors,
which propel the rest of humanity,
do not register on the yogi's consciousness.

कृत्यं किमपि नैवास्ति न कापि हृदि रञ्जना ।
kṛtyaṁ kimapi naivāsti na kāpi hṛdi rañjanā ,
यथा जीवनमेवेह जीवन्मुक्तस्य योगिनः ॥ १८-१३ ॥
yathā jīvanameveha jīvanmuktasya yoginaḥ (18-13)

The *Jīvan-mukta* Yogi
—he who has managed to attain emancipation with the body
still intact—
continues to operate so long as the body still remains attached;

but his actions are mere appearances,
because for him there is neither obligating duties nor attachments.
The arrows of past karmas might still direct and propel his body forward
—till their impetus is spent—
but his heart is never attached to anything of the world.

क्व मोहः क्व च वा विश्वं क्व तद् ध्यानं क्व मुक्तता ।
kva mohaḥ kva ca vā viśvaṁ kva tad dhyānaṁ kva muktatā ,
सर्वसङ्कल्पसीमायां विश्रान्तस्य महात्मनः ॥१८-१४॥
sarvasaṅkalpasīmāyāṁ viśrāntasya mahātmanaḥ (18-14)

For the great soul who has stepped across the threshold of creation's bounds
—across the dividing line and into the realm of the Unmanifest—
...who has come to repose
within the realm of the Singularity,
beyond the realm of conceptions and desires—
where is delusion?
where the universe and its renunciation?
where the notions of sitting in meditations
or attaining liberation?

येन विश्वमिदं दृष्टं स नास्तीति करोतु वै ।
yena viśvamidaṁ dṛṣṭaṁ sa nāstīti karotu vai ,
निर्वासनः किं कुरुते पश्यन्नपि न पश्यति ॥१८-१५॥
nirvāsanaḥ kiṁ kurute paśyannapi na paśyati (18-15)

He who sees the universe
might try to make efforts to negate or evade it;
but what possible thing is necessitated unto the yogi who sees only Oneness,
even though the universe in all its manifoldness
is continually impinging on his eyes?
...who has gone beyond all effort, inclination, desire?

He may see,
but there's only the act of eyesight in itself—
it provokes no thought,
it remains unmixed of anything produced from within the mind
in response.

येन दृष्टं परं ब्रह्म सोऽहं ब्रह्मेति चिन्तयेत् ।
yena dṛṣṭaṁ paraṁ brahma so'haṁ brahmeti cintayet ,
किं चिन्तयति निश्चिन्तो द्वितीयं यो न पश्यति ॥ १८-१६ ॥
kiṁ cintayati niścinto dvitīyaṁ yo na paśyati (18-16)

He who has heard of the supreme reality Brahama attempts
meditation thinking "I am Brahama".
But he who has directly realized Brahama,
he who see no other second other than The-One,
who is unable to detect duality anywhere
—what can that sage
possibly engage his thoughts in?

दृष्टो येनात्मविक्षेपो निरोधं कुरुते त्वसौ ।
dṛṣṭo yenātmavikṣepo nirodhaṁ kurute tvasau ,
उदारस्तु न विक्षिप्तः साध्याभावात्करोति किम् ॥ १८-१७॥
udārastu na vikṣiptaḥ sādhyābhāvātkaroti kim (18-17)

He, by whom inner distractions are perceived,
may put an end to them by the act of exercising control.
But the exalted soul finds nothing distracting him
—seeing only the same Oneness everywhere, inside and out—
so what acts of control need he perform?
...and to remove what?

धीरो लोकविपर्यस्तो वर्तमानोऽपि लोकवत् ।
dhīro lokaviparyasto vartamāno'pi lokavat ,
न समाधिं न विक्षेपं न लोपं स्वस्य पश्यति ॥ १८-१८॥
na samādhiṁ na vikṣepaṁ na lopaṁ svasya paśyati (18-18)

Although, on the outside an exalted sage appears to be just like
the rest,
but from within he is the very opposite.
He perceives no troubles distracting him;

he perceives no taints or defilements in his persona he needs to rectify,
and he find no necessity
to be absorbed in Samadhi either.

भावाभावविहीनो यस्तृप्तो निर्वासनो बुधः ।
bhāvābhāvavihīno yastṛpto nirvāsano budhaḥ ,
नैव किञ्चित्कृतं तेन लोकदृष्ट्या विकुर्वता ॥ १८-१९ ॥
naiva kiñcitkṛtaṁ tena lokadṛṣṭyā vikurvatā (18-19)

Dwelling in the realm of non-duality,
freed of all wants and desires,
the sage is not awake
to the existence or non-existence of the universe.
Ever wise and ever satisfied,
he does nothing at all
—always staying beyond karma's bounds
...even though in the eyes of the world
he is seen performing work.

प्रवृत्तौ वा निवृत्तौ वा नैव धीरस्य दुर्ग्रहः ।
pravṛttau vā nivṛttau vā naiva dhīrasya durgrahaḥ ,
यदा यत्कर्तुमायाति तत्कृत्वा तिष्ठतः सुखम् ॥ १८-२० ॥
yadā yatkartumāyāti tatkṛtvā tiṣṭhataḥ sukham (18-20)

The sage abides ever experiencing the bliss of his innate essence.
Unperturbed and always tranquil,
he neither gravitates nor flees
—from activity or inactivity.
He does naturally what comes to him;
and whatever come to be done by him,
he is never driven to achieve it;
for he finds himself perfect and pure,
in lack of nothing for which he needs to strive.

निर्वासनो निरालम्बः स्वच्छन्दो मुक्तबन्धनः ।
nirvāsano nirālambaḥ svacchando muktabandhanaḥ ,
क्षिप्तः संस्कारवातेन चेष्टते शुष्कपर्णवत् ॥ १८-२१ ॥
kṣiptaḥ saṁskāravātena ceṣṭate śuṣkaparṇavat (18-21)

Desireless, self-sufficient,
sovereign, carefree, free of bondages
—the sage abides wherever the impetus of his *Prārabdha* places him
...moving without resistance
...without imposing his own will
—like a dead leaf drifting hither, thither
in the winds of causality of karmas
from this life and prior.

असंसारस्य तु क्वापि न हर्षो न विषादता ।
asaṁsārasya tu kvāpi na harṣo na viṣādatā ,
स शीतलमना नित्यं विदेह इव राजये ॥ १८-२२ ॥
sa śītalamanā nityaṁ videha iva rājaye (18-22)

Enlightened in the knowledge of the Self,
he transcends all worldly life,
and for him there is neither joy nor sorrow.
Ever of a serene countenance
the yogi lives only as the Ātmā—
as if perfectly detached from the body and mind.

कुत्रापि न जिहासास्ति नाशो वापि न कुत्रचित् ।
kutrāpi na jihāsāsti nāśo vāpi na kutracit ,
आत्मारामस्य धीरस्य शीतलाच्छतरात्मनः ॥ १८-२३ ॥
ātmārāmasya dhīrasya śītalācchatarātmanaḥ (18-23)

Whose only joy abides in the Self, and who
—by dint of the perfection and completeness of the Ātmā—
thus abides always serene and pure,
within and without
—he finds no need to renounce anything;

he finds no defilements to get rid of,
and he has no wish to acquire anything
—because he lives as the Ātmā-Rāma,
ever perfect, ever in peace.

प्रकृत्या शून्यचित्तस्य कुर्वतोऽस्य यदृच्छया ।
prakṛtyā śūnyacittasya kurvato'sya yadṛcchayā ,
प्राकृतस्येव धीरस्य न मानो नावमानता ॥ १८-२४॥
prākṛtasyeva dhīrasya na māno nāvamānatā (18-24)

Abiding naturally as the Self
—unmodified pristine consciousness,
with the mind rendered dissolved—
the sage acts out from a natural innocence;
and for him there are no such thing as honor and humiliation,
such as exist in the world of beings.

कृतं देहेन कर्मेदं न मया शुद्धरूपिणा ।
kṛtaṁ dehena karmedaṁ na mayā śuddharūpiṇā ,
इति चिन्तानुरोधी यः कुर्वन्नपि करोति न ॥ १८-२५॥
iti cintānurodhī yaḥ kurvannapi karoti na (18-25)

Acting in conformity with unfeigned stance of pureness that seems to aver:
"the body alone acts and not I—
who am the pristine Self, the non-doer,"
the sage in fact performs no karmas from the mind
—even though visibly seen engaged in activity.

अतद्वादीव कुरुते न भवेदपि बालिशः ।
atadvādīva kurute na bhavedapi bāliśaḥ ,
जीवन्मुक्तः सुखी श्रीमान् संसरन्नपि शोभते ॥ १८-२६ ॥
jīvanmuktaḥ sukhī śrīmān saṁsarannapi śobhate (18-26)

The *Jīvan-mukta*
—one who is liberated though still abiding in a body—
may appear to do things without a motive or a purpose to show—alike some fool—
...but he is the real wise.

Although engaged in karma,
he goes beyond karma's bounds,
and is able to abide in unqualified happiness,
unconcerned with what fruits actions bring
...or do not bring.

नानाविचारसुश्रान्तो धीरो विश्रान्तिमागतः ।
nānāvicārasuśrānto dhīro viśrāntimāgataḥ ,
न कल्पते न जाति न श्रृणोति न पश्यति ॥१८-२७॥
na kalpate na jāti na śṛṇoti na paśyati (18-27)

Weary of conflicting ideologies of the world reasoned out in divergent ways,
the wise
—having enough of ideas and debates—
has decided, "enough already!"
He simply dwells in the serenity of the Ātmā,
without expending the exertion
to hear, see, imagine, know.

असमाधेरविक्षेपान् न मुमुक्षुर्न चेतरः ।
asamādheravikṣepān na mumukṣurna cetaraḥ ,
निश्चित्य कल्पितं पश्यन् ब्रह्मैवास्ते महाशयः ॥१८-२८॥
niścitya kalpitaṁ paśyan brahmaivāste mahāśayaḥ (18-28)

That exalted sage...
—who has known the universe to be a figment even though perceiving it with senses
—who has risen above notions such as mental distractions or making the mind still in meditations
—who neither desires nor shuns liberation ...or its opposite,
abides only as One in Brahama,
here, now, and forever.

यस्यान्तः स्यादहङ्कारो न करोति करोति सः ।
yasyāntaḥ syādahaṅkāro na karoti karoti saḥ ,
निरहङ्कारधीरेण न किञ्चिदकृतं कृतम् ॥१८-२९॥
nirahaṅkāradhīreṇa na kiñcidakṛtaṁ kṛtam (18-29)

He, who remains rooted to the ego,
always remains fettered by the karma's bonds
even though not actually performing work
—because he is thoroughly attached
and has enacted them already in the mind.
But the steadfast sage
—void of the ideas of 'me' and 'mine',
who abides only as the Self—
remains unsullied of karma's effects,
even though seen visibly engaged in action.

नोद्विग्नं न च सन्तुष्टमकर्तृ स्पन्दवर्जितम् ।
nodvignaṁ na ca santuṣṭamakartṛ spandavarjitam ,
निराशं गतसन्देहं चित्तं मुक्तस्य राजते ॥ १८-३० ॥
nirāśaṁ gatasandehaṁ cittaṁ muktasya rājate (18-30)

The consciousness of the liberated sage
becomes neither agitated nor delighted;
It shines fiery only as Itself—
actionless, motionless, desireless,
and doubtlessly free of incertitudes.

निर्ध्यातुं चेष्टितुं वापि यच्चित्तं न प्रवर्तते ।
nirdhyātuṁ ceṣṭituṁ vāpi yaccittaṁ na pravartate ,
निर्निमित्तमिदं किन्तु निर्ध्यायेति विचेष्टते ॥ १८-३१ ॥
nirnimittamidaṁ kintu nirdhyāyeti viceṣṭate (18-31)

For the liberated sage,
there is no mind which sets out to pursue meditation
or to indulge in worldly acts.
Free of exertions
—with his mind, for the most part, staying dissolved,
crystallizing in and out—
the consciousness of the sage is very much
rich and active,
and he dwells in a meditative stance naturally
—unprompted and with no motive to serve.

तत्त्वं यथार्थमाकर्ण्य मन्दः प्राप्नोति मूढताम् ।
tattvaṁ yathārthamākarṇya mandaḥ prāpnoti mūḍhatām ,
अथवा याति सङ्कोचममूढः कोऽपि मूढवत् ॥ १८-३२ ॥
athavā yāti saṅkocamamūḍhaḥ ko'pi mūḍhavat (18-32)

A dull-witted soul becomes perplexed
hearing the Truth of the Ātmā;
but upon hearing the same Truth,
the more intelligent understands and acts in accordance with it,
and consequently he retreats within himself as a result of that
—in fact becoming just like some dull person
on the outside.

एकाग्रता निरोधो वा मूढैरभ्यस्यते भृशम् ।
ekāgratā nirodho vā mūḍhairabhyasyate bhṛśam ,
धीराः कृत्यं न पश्यन्ति सुप्तवत्स्वपदे स्थिताः ॥ १८-३३ ॥
dhīrāḥ kṛtyaṁ na paśyanti suptavatsvapade sthitāḥ (18-33)

The unwitting man is continually engaged
—practicing mind controls and concentrations
[but alas, bereft of the science of Self-Knowledge].
In direct contrast,
the wise finds nothing he needs to do
—since he always abides as the Ātmā,
outwardly just like a dullard in deep sleep.

अप्रयत्नात् प्रयत्नाद्वा मूढो नाप्नोति निर्वृतिम् ।
aprayatnāt prayatnād vā mūḍho nāpnoti nirvṛtim ,
तत्त्वनिश्चयमात्रेण प्राज्ञो भवति निर्वृतः ॥ १८-३४ ॥
tattvaniścayamātreṇa prājño bhavati nirvṛtaḥ (18-34)

The ignorant person does not find peace—
either by action or by renunciation of action.
In direct contrast the wise person,
—simply from knowing the Truth of Ātmā and pursuing that
Truth to become one in the Ātmā—
always remains in peace and happiness
...regardless if his body is performing action or no action.

शुद्धं बुद्धं प्रियं पूर्णं निष्प्रपञ्चं निरामयम् ।
śuddhaṁ buddhaṁ priyaṁ pūrṇaṁ niṣprapañcaṁ nirāmayam ,
आत्मानं तं न जानन्ति तत्राभ्यासपरा जनाः ॥ १८-३५ ॥
ātmānaṁ taṁ na jānanti tatrābhyāsaparā janāḥ (18-35)

Though pursuing various rituals and practices,
still men do not find the Ātmā
—which is pure intelligence, most adorable, arrantly perfect and complete, beyond any evil, beyond anything of the world.
The Ātmā,
being of the nature of Intelligence,
is therefore the subject of knowledge and realization,
and not of physical practices and actions.

नाप्नोति कर्मणा मोक्षं विमूढोऽभ्यासरूपिणा ।
nāpnoti karmaṇā mokṣaṁ vimūḍho'bhyāsarūpiṇā ,
धन्यो विज्ञानमात्रेण मुक्तस्तिष्ठत्यविक्रियः ॥ १८-३६ ॥
dhanyo vijñānamātreṇa muktastiṣṭhatyavikriyaḥ (18-36)

Though repeatedly exerting
—engaged in practices of mind-control and concentrations—
still the ignorant person
—who is bereft of Self-Knowledge—
does not attain liberation;
whereas the blessed wise abides liberated naturally
—merely by dint of Self-Knowledge—
even though he remains innocent of all such exertions.

मूढो नाप्नोति तद् ब्रह्म यतो भवितुमिच्छति ।
mūḍho nāpnoti tad brahma yato bhavitumicchati ,
अनिच्छन्नपि धीरो हि परब्रह्मस्वरूपभाक् ॥ १८-३७ ॥
anicchannapi dhīro hi parabrahmasvarūpabhāk (18-37)

The ignorant person does not attain Brahama
—for he so yearns to attain It.
That desire itself
—along with the inherent notion of duality and separation which one carries—
becoming an impediment on the way.

The wise sage simply becomes one in
Brahama-Rāma naturally,
even without desiring to do so
—because having rejected notions of separation and dualities through Self-Knowledge,
he already stands established in that Supreme.

-*-

निराधारा ग्रहव्यग्रा मूढाः संसारपोषकाः ।
nirādhārā grahavyagrā mūḍhāḥ saṁsāraposakāḥ ,
एतस्यानर्थमूलस्य मूलच्छेदः कृतो बुधैः ॥१८-३८॥
etasyānarthamūlasya mūlacchedaḥ kṛto budhaiḥ (18-38)

-*-

Yearning for freedom from the world
—but bereft of the support of Knowledge of Self—
the ignorant man only ends up further sustaining duality,
keeping the variegated universe alive.
The wise
—with the aid of Self-Knowledge and in firm embrace of non-duality—
is able to sever away at the very root of the universe,
which is the fount of every misery.

-*-

न शान्तिं लभते मूढो यतः शमितुमिच्छति ।
na śāntiṁ labhate mūḍho yataḥ śamitumicchati ,
धीरस्तत्त्वं विनिश्चित्य सर्वदा शान्तमानसः ॥१८-३९॥
dhīrastattvaṁ viniścitya sarvadā śāntamānasaḥ (18-39)

-*-

The fool yearns for peace and engages in practices like mind-control etc.,
—and consequently he cannot attain peace.
The steadfast wise,
who knows the Truth of the Non-dual One-Existence and has realized that Ātmā,
always abides in a tranquil state
naturally.

क्वात्मनो दर्शनं तस्य यद् दृष्टमवलम्बते ।
kvātmano darśanaṁ tasya yad dṛṣṭamavalambate ,
धीरास्तं तं न पश्यन्ति पश्यन्त्यात्मानमव्ययम् ॥ १८-४० ॥
dhīrāstaṁ taṁ na paśyanti paśyantyātmānamavyayam (18-40)

Where is Self-Knowledge for him whose knowledge arises from a material framework:
name, words, forms, external things?
The wise does not see or think 'this' and 'that'
Firmly established in non-duality,
he perceives just the One Immutable Reality:
the Param-Ātmā-Rāma.

क्व निरोधो विमूढस्य यो निर्बन्धं करोति वै ।
kva nirodho vimūḍhasya yo nirbandhaṁ karoti vai ,
स्वारामस्यैव धीरस्य सर्वदासावकृत्रिमः ॥ १८-४१ ॥
svārāmasyaiva dhīrasya sarvadāsāvakṛtrimaḥ (18-41)

Where can be mind-control and happiness
for the deluded ignorant soul
who so desperately strives for it
(—but without resorting to Self-Knowledge first)?
But it is the natural state of the steadfast soul
whose only joy is the Ātmā-Rāma.

भावस्य भावकः कश्चिन् न किञ्चिद् भावकोपरः ।
bhāvasya bhāvakaḥ kaścin na kiñcid bhāvakoparaḥ ,
उभयाभावकः कश्चिद् एवमेव निराकुलः ॥ १८-४२ ॥
ubhayābhāvakaḥ kaścid evameva nirākulaḥ (18-42)

There are some who think that this show of fluxing phenomena exists,
and there are others who reason that nothing exists.
Rare indeed is the wise sage who takes neither stance,
who remains quiet
staying beyond deliberations,
simply abiding in the non-duality of the Self
...enjoying peace.

शुद्धमद्वयमात्मानं भावयन्ति कुबुद्धयः ।
śuddhamadvayamātmānaṁ bhāvayanti kubuddhayaḥ ,
न तु जानन्ति संमोहाद्यावज्जीवमनिर्वृताः ॥ १८-४३॥
na tu jānanti saṁmohādyāvajjīvamanirvṛtāḥ (18-43)

The dull witted have heard of the Ātmā-Rāma
—the pure, the One without a second.
But alas!
deluded by Rāma's Māyā
—still not having made that realization their own direct personal experience—
they continue under the subjugations of worldly sufferings
so long as they live.

मुमुक्षोर्बुद्धिरालम्बमन्तरेण न विद्यते ।
mumukṣorbuddhirālambamantareṇa na vidyate ,
निरालम्बैव निष्कामा बुद्धिर्मुक्तस्य सर्वदा ॥ १८-४४॥
nirālambaiva niṣkāmā buddhirmuktasya sarvadā (18-44)

The mind that yearns for liberation
remains far from attaining it
—being that the mind which yearns,
still abides and functions.
Whereas the consciousness of the wise sage innately abides in freedom
—free of longings, independent of the mind—
which mind in fact has dried up and died.

विषयद्वीपिनो वीक्ष्य चकिताः शरणार्थिनः ।
viṣayadvīpino vīkṣya cakitāḥ śaraṇārthinaḥ ,
विशन्ति झटिति क्रोडं निरोधैकाग्रसिद्धये ॥ १८-४५॥
viśanti jhaṭiti kroḍaṁ nirodhaikāgrasiddhaye (18-45)

Confronted with the formidable objects of the senses,
the frightened soul sees them as terrible tigers,
and trembling with fear
he forthwith takes flight to the deep cave of contemplation
—to find shelter and gain self-control.

निर्वासनं हरिं दृष्ट्वा तूष्णीं विषयदन्तिनः ।
nirvāsanaṁ hariṁ dṛṣṭvā tūṣṇīṁ viṣayadantinaḥ ,
पलायन्ते न शक्तास्ते सेवन्ते कृतचाटवः ॥ १८-४६ ॥
palāyante na śaktāste sevante kṛtacāṭavaḥ (18-46)

But those same sense-objects
—when they see a lion in the shape of a desireless man—
turn into frightened little elephants
...and they quietly take to their heels,
or
—if unable to turn tail—
they serve him like fawning adulators.

न मुक्तिकारिकां धत्ते निःशङ्को युक्तमानसः ।
na muktikārikāṁ dhatte niḥśaṅko yuktamānasaḥ ,
पश्यन् शृण्वन् स्पृशन् जिघ्रन्नश्नन्नास्ते यथासुखम् ॥ १८-४७॥
paśyan śṛṇvan spṛśan jighrannaśnannāste yathāsukham (18-47)

Whose doubts stand resolved,
whose mind is merged within the Self
—he has no need to resort to practicing of mind-control as the means to liberation.
He lives contented even when engaged in outward activities
like seeing, hearing, touching, smelling, eating
—because with his mind dissolved
he naturally abides in the bliss of the Ātmā-Rāma at all times.

वस्तुश्रवणमात्रेण शुद्धबुद्धिर्निराकुलः ।
vastuśravaṇamātreṇa śuddhabuddhirnirākulaḥ ,
नैवाचारमनाचारमौदास्यं वा प्रपश्यति ॥ १८-४८॥
naivācāramanācāramaudāsyaṁ vā prapaśyati (18-48)

The self-realized wise sage
—who, out of perfection,
is able to instantly reach the state of perfect tranquility by merely hearing the word—
goes beyond the enjoined rules of conduct;

because then he can no longer fathom what is proper action,
or what improper,
or even the difference between action and inaction.

यदा यत्कर्तुमायाति तदा तत्कुरुते ऋजुः ।
yadā yatkartumāyāti tadā tatkurute ṛjuḥ ,
शुभं वाप्यशुभं वापि तस्य चेष्टा हि बालवत् ॥ १८-४९ ॥
śubhaṁ vāpyaśubhaṁ vāpi tasya ceṣṭā hi bālavat (18-49)

In that exalted state,
the sage does whatever comes to be done by him innocently and naturally
—whether deemed by others to be good or bad,
whether seen as auspicious or inauspicious;
for his actions are like those of a child,
born of the state of pure innocence.

स्वातन्त्र्यात्सुखमाप्नोति स्वातन्त्र्याल्लभते परम् ।
svātantryātsukhamāpnoti svātantryāllabhate param ,
स्वातन्त्र्यान्निर्वृतिं गच्छेत्स्वातन्त्र्यात् परमं पदम् ॥ १८-५० ॥
svātantryānnirvṛtiṁ gacchetsvātantryāt paramaṁ padam (18-50)

Freedom is the key:
freedom from the universe,
freedom from duality,
freedom from the mind.
That freedom leads to happiness,
that freedom leads to one's own Self,
that freedom leads to untroubled peace:
ultimately leading to that sovereign state
where nothing else remains
to be sought or gained.

अकर्तृत्वमभोक्तृत्वं स्वात्मनो मन्यते यदा ।
akartṛtvamabhoktṛtvaṁ svātmano manyate yadā ,
तदा क्षीणा भवन्त्येव समस्ताश्चित्तवृत्तयः ॥ १८-५१ ॥
tadā kṣīṇā bhavantyeva samastāścittavṛttayaḥ (18-51)

Having realized—
"I am neither the doer, nor the partaker,"
—all modifications of the consciousness stand dissolved;
the mind dries up and dies
and the pristine Self shines as Itself,
in all its fiery effulgence.

उच्छृङ्खलाप्यकृतिका स्थितिर्धीरस्य राजते ।
ucchṛṅkhalāpyakṛtikā sthitirdhīrasya rājate ,
न तु सस्पृहचित्तस्य शान्तिर्मूढस्य कृत्रिमा ॥ १८-५२ ॥
na tu saspṛhacittasya śāntirmūḍhasya kṛtrimā (18-52)

The fool,
his mind full of desires,
can only simulate a sham of calmness;
whereas the fiery calm of the steadfast wise,
whose conduct is unrestricted by
selfish motive, pretense, guile,
shines naturally resplendent.

विलसन्ति महाभोगैर्विशन्ति गिरिगह्वरान् ।
vilasanti mahābhogairviśanti girigahvarān ,
निरस्तकल्पना धीरा अबद्धा मुक्तबुद्धयः ॥ १८-५३ ॥
nirastakalpanā dhīrā abaddhā muktabuddhayaḥ (18-53)

Those of steady wisdom
—who have transcended the mind and therefore abide in freedom—
simply disport in the world,
sometimes engaged in varying pastimes,
or at times retreating into deep mountain caves.

श्रोत्रियं देवतां तीर्थमङ्गनां भूपतिं प्रियम् ।
śrotriyaṁ devatāṁ tīrthamaṅganāṁ bhūpatiṁ priyam ,
दृष्ट्वा सम्पूज्य धीरस्य न कापि हृदि वासना ॥ १८-५४ ॥
dṛṣṭvā sampūjya dhīrasya na kāpi hṛdi vāsanā (18-54)

In the heart of the steady wise,
there arises no desire whatsoever, anywhere, anytime
—whether he is honoring a person versed in sacred lore,
or venerating gods and holy places,
or seeing a lovely woman,
or a king,
or his own kin.

भृत्यैः पुत्रैः कलत्रैश्च दौहित्रैश्चापि गोत्रजैः ।
bhṛtyaiḥ putraiḥ kalatraiśca dauhitraiścāpi gotrajaiḥ ,
विहस्य धिक्कृतो योगी न याति विकृतिं मनाक् ॥ १८-५५॥
vihasya dhikkṛto yogī na yāti vikṛtiṁ manāk (18-55)

The yogi remains unperturbed and tranquil
even when ridiculed, reproached, despised
—even if by his own subordinate, spouse, kin, child, grandchild.
His consciousness undergoes no modification from anything
...nay, not in the least.

सन्तुष्टोऽपि न सन्तुष्टः खिन्नोऽपि न च खिद्यते ।
santuṣṭo'pi na santuṣṭaḥ khinno'pi na ca khidyate ,
तस्याश्चर्यदशां तां तां तादृशा एव जानते ॥ १८-५६॥
tasyāścaryadaśāṁ tāṁ tāṁ tādṛśā eva jānate (18-56)

Though placed amidst delights,
he suffers no pleasures;
although put to pain, he suffers no misery.
Only those who themselves have reached that exalted state
can understand that wonderful state of consciousness.

कर्तव्यतैव संसारो न तां पश्यन्ति सूरयः ।
kartavyataiva saṁsāro na tāṁ paśyanti sūrayaḥ ,
शून्याकारा निराकारा निर्विकारा निरामयाः ॥ १८-५७॥
śūnyākārā nirākārā nirvikārā nirāmayāḥ (18-57)

The sense of obligating duty belongs in the world of relative existence,
and it only strengthens the notions of duality
—and therefore the wise gives no credence to it.

Having realized himself to be
the formless untainted immutable
all-pervasive Consciousness,
the sage transcends all ordained duties.

अकुर्वन्नपि सङ्क्षोभाद् व्यग्रः सर्वत्र मूढधीः ।
akurvannapi saṅkṣobhād vyagraḥ sarvatra mūḍhadhīḥ ,
कुर्वन्नपि तु कृत्यानि कुशलो हि निराकुलः ॥ १८-५८ ॥
kurvannapi tu kṛtyāni kuśalo hi nirākulaḥ (18-58)

Even when not doing anything,
an unintelligent person remains frantic and agitated—
ever so vexed by little distractions.
In dire contrast,
one who is skilful and wise,
remains tranquil and unperturbed always
even when engaged in intense activity.

सुखमास्ते सुखं शेते सुखमायाति याति च ।
sukhamāste sukhaṁ śete sukhamāyāti yāti ca ,
सुखं वक्ति सुखं भुङ्क्ते व्यवहारेऽपि शान्तधीः ॥ १८-५९ ॥
sukhaṁ vakti sukhaṁ bhuṅkte vyavahāre'pi śāntadhīḥ (18-59)

Contented he sits,
contented he lies down,
contented he comes and goes and moves about,
and happily he speaks and eats
—and this way abiding in contentedness
in all his dealings with the world,
the wise one remains ever at peace.

स्वभावाद्यस्य नैवार्तिर्लोकवद् व्यवहारिणः ।
svabhāvādyasya naivārtirlokavad vyavahāriṇaḥ ,
महाहृद इवाक्षोभ्यो गतक्लेशः सुशोभते ॥ १८-६० ॥
mahāhṛda ivākṣobhyo gatakleśaḥ suśobhate (18-60)

By virtue of his realization as the Self,
he who indeed remains undistressed
even when navigating the ordinary course of human affairs
—who abides tranquil like the calm surface of a great lake—

verily he shines splendorous,
with all his sorrows dissipated.

निवृत्तिरपि मूढस्य प्रवृत्ति रुपजायते ।
nivṛttirapi mūḍhasya pravṛtti rupajāyate ,
प्रवृत्तिरपि धीरस्य निवृत्तिफलभागिनी ॥ १८-६१ ॥
pravṛttirapi dhīrasya nivṛttiphalabhāginī (18-61)

From even the passive, inactive life of a deluded person,
there sprouts forth an upheaval of activity;
whereas from the activity of one
who is intelligent and steadfast,
there ensues only the sweet fruit of inaction.

परिग्रहेषु वैराग्यं प्रायो मूढस्य दृश्यते ।
parigraheṣu vairāgyaṁ prāyo mūḍhasya dṛśyate ,
देहे विगलिताशस्य क्व रागः क्व विरागता ॥ १८-६२ ॥
dehe vigalitāśasya kva rāgaḥ kva virāgatā (18-62)

The deluded man may often display aversion for possessions—
pledging to renounce it all.
As to the wise
—whose ownership and expectations have melted away even
with respect to his own body—
where is that which ought to be renounced?
...where any desires and aversions that need giving up?

भावनाभावनासक्ता दृष्टिर्मूढस्य सर्वदा ।
bhāvanābhāvanāsaktā dṛṣṭirmūḍhasya sarvadā ,
भाव्यभावनया सा तु स्वस्थस्यादृष्टिरूपिणी ॥ १८-६३ ॥
bhāvyabhāvanayā sā tu svasthasyādṛṣṭirūpiṇī (18-63)

The deluded man is always with considerations
...having opinion and attitude towards everything,
such as for-against, give-take etc.
But the consciousness of the wise,
although attended with thinking,
transcends all opposites.

Neither for, nor against,
he abides simply and naturally
—as awareness pure.

सर्वारम्भेषु निष्कामो यश्चरेद् बालवन् मुनिः ।
sarvārambheṣu niṣkāmo yaścared bālavan muniḥ ,
न लेपस्तस्य शुद्धस्य क्रियमाणेऽपि कर्मणि ॥ १८-६४॥
na lepastasya śuddhasya kriyamāṇe'pi karmaṇi (18-64)

Even though outwardly engaged in action,
the wise sage remains perfectly detached
—like a child engaged in an innocent play.
Bereft of any personal motive to serve
he remains detached and separated from the work he may be seen apparently engaged in.

स एव धन्य आत्मज्ञः सर्वभावेषु यः समः ।
sa eva dhanya ātmajñaḥ sarvabhāveṣu yaḥ samaḥ ,
पश्यन् शृण्वन् स्पृशन् जिघ्रन् अश्नन्निस्तर्षमानसः ॥ १८-६५॥
paśyan śṛṇvan spṛśan jighrann aśnannistarṣamānasaḥ (18-65)

Blessed is the sage
who dwells abiding in the pristineness of the Ātmā
—whatever the circumstance—
ever equanimous whatever he may be doing
—seeing, hearing, touching, smelling, eating—
always in sameness.

क्व संसारः क्व चाभासः क्व साध्यं क्व च साधनम् ।
kva saṁsāraḥ kva cābhāsaḥ kva sādhyaṁ kva ca sādhanam ,
आकाशस्येव धीरस्य निर्विकल्पस्य सर्वदा ॥ १८-६६॥
ākāśasyeva dhīrasya nirvikalpasya sarvadā (18-66)

Where the world that's in a flux?
Whither the show of changing things?
What's the purpose worth striving for?
...and what the means for attaining it?
Unto the wise sage who abides changeless like the firmament,
such questions just echo back from his infinite depth
without an answer.

स जयत्यर्थसंन्यासी पूर्णस्वरसविग्रहः ।
sa jayatyarthasaṁnyāsī pūrṇasvarasavigrahaḥ ,
अकृत्रिमोऽनवच्छिन्ने समाधिर्यस्य वर्तते ॥ १८-६७॥
akṛtrimo'navacchinne samādhiryasya vartate (18-67)

Glory be to the *Sanyāsī*
—free of desires and established in his innate nature—
the very embodiment of infinite bliss.
Verily he spontaneously abides in the highest state of *Samādhi*,
because he has become one with The-One.

बहुनात्र किमुक्तेन ज्ञाततत्त्वो महाशयः ।
bahunātra kimuktena jñātatattvo mahāśayaḥ ,
भोगमोक्षनिराकाङ्क्षी सदा सर्वत्र नीरसः ॥ १८-६८॥
bhogamokṣanirākāṅkṣī sadā sarvatra nīrasaḥ (18-68)

To put it succinctly:
the great soul who has realized the Ātmā—
he becomes free from all wants;
he craves neither enjoyments nor even emancipation;
and everywhere and at all times,
he abides unfettered, aloof, unconcerned
...and ever blissful.

महदादि जगद्द्वैतं नाममात्रविजृम्भितम् ।
mahadādi jagaddvaitaṁ nāmamātravijṛmbhitam ,
विहाय शुद्धबोधस्य किं कृत्यमवशिष्यते ॥ १८-६९॥
vihāya śuddhabodhasya kiṁ kṛtyamavaśiṣyate (18-69)

Unto the enlightened sage,
the entirety of Existence
—ranging from the immense expanse of the Unmanifest Reality
to the multiplicity of the manifest universe—
is nothing but a montage of divergent names.
What really is there which remains to be done by that sage who has withdrawn from it all,
who now simply abides as the Ātmā-Rāma
—arrantly perfect and pure?

भ्रमभूतमिदं सर्वं किञ्चिन्नास्तीति निश्चयी ।
bhramabhūtamidaṁ sarvaṁ kiñcinnāstīti niścayī ,
अलक्ष्यस्फुरणः शुद्धः स्वभावेनैव शाम्यति ॥ १८-७० ॥
alakṣyasphuraṇaḥ śuddhaḥ svabhāvenaiva śāmyati (18-70)

All this is but a magician's illusion playing out
—here for a moment and gone the next.
That which Really exists
—always has been, and ever will—
is just the Param-Ātmā-Rāma,
the One-Consciousness, the Singularity,
the only Reality.

To whom that inexpressible Reality
—the Ātmā-Rāma—
is realized to be he himself,
he naturally enjoys the everlasting bliss of his innate essence.

शुद्धस्फुरणरूपस्य दृश्यभावमपश्यतः ।
śuddhasphuraṇarūpasya dṛśyabhāvamapaśyataḥ ,
क्व विधिः क्व च वैराग्यं क्व त्यागः क्व शमोऽपि वा ॥ १८-७१ ॥
kva vidhiḥ kva ca vairāgyaṁ kva tyāgaḥ kva śamo'pi vā (18-71)

For him who abides as pure consciousness
—for whom the manifest universe is but a dream,
void of objective reality—
what rules of conduct need apply?
For one who is already ever-pure ever-free,
wherefore the notions of restraint, dispassion, renunciation?

स्फुरतोऽनन्तरूपेण प्रकृतिं च न पश्यतः ।
sphurato'nantarūpeṇa prakṛtiṁ ca na paśyataḥ ,
क्व बन्धः क्व च वा मोक्षः क्व हर्षः क्व विषादिता ॥ १८-७२ ॥
kva bandhaḥ kva ca vā mokṣaḥ kva harṣaḥ kva viṣāditā (18-72)

For one who perceiveth no relative existence
—who shines fiery in his resplendent glory as Infinite
Existence—
...where is bondage?

...and where and from whom liberation?
...and where exist jovialities?
...and where grief?

बुद्धिपर्यन्तसंसारे मायामात्रं विवर्तते ।
buddhiparyantasaṁsāre māyāmātraṁ vivartate ,
निर्ममो निरहङ्कारो निष्कामः शोभते बुधः ॥ १८-७३ ॥
nirmamo nirahaṅkāro niṣkāmaḥ śobhate budhaḥ (18-73)

The universe is an apparition
—a web of delusions spun out by Rāma's Māyā;
and in the fiery glow of Self-Knowledge,
the universe vanishes just like a dream it was.
Then,
bereft of the sense of 'I', and 'mine',
and minus all attachments,
the sage continues in that dream
as long as
the dream will show.

अक्षयं गतसन्तापमात्मानं पश्यतो मुनेः ।
akṣayaṁ gatasantāpamātmānaṁ paśyato muneḥ ,
क्व विद्या च क्व वा विश्वं क्व देहोऽहं ममेति वा ॥ १८-७४ ॥
kva vidyā ca kva vā viśvaṁ kva deho'haṁ mameti vā (18-74)

The sage
—who knows himself as the imperishable Self,
the Self of all—
suffers no grief;
for him all notions dissolve.
...and then,
where and what is knowledge and science?
...and what the universe?
...and where the feeling that 'I am the body',
or that 'the body is mine'?

निरोधादीनि कर्माणि जहाति जडधीर्यदि ।
nirodhādīni karmāṇi jahāti jaḍadhīryadi ,
मनोरथान् प्रलापांश्च कर्तुमाप्नोत्यतत्क्षणात् ॥ १८-७५ ॥
manorathān pralāpāṁśca kartumāpnotyatatkṣaṇāt (18-75)

He who is ensnared in dualities
—one who has not realized the Self—
that ignorant person cannot afford to relinquish control over the mind,
or give up his spiritual practices;
because the moment he does so,
he immediately falls down from his spiritual path
...falling prey to desires, fancies, delusions.

मन्दः श्रुत्वापि तद्वस्तु न जहाति विमूढताम् ।
mandaḥ śrutvāpi tadvastu na jahāti vimūḍhatām ,
निर्विकल्पो बहिर्यत्नादन्तर्विषयलालसः ॥ १८-७६ ॥
nirvikalpo bahiryatnādantarviṣayalālasaḥ (18-76)

The stupe,
even after hearing of the Ātmā, the highest Truth,
still continues clinging to his delusions;
and although with some effort
he manages to display some sense of peace for a little while,
but desires for the sense-enjoyments never really leave his heart,
and sooner or later he falls prey to them.

ज्ञानाद् गलितकर्मा यो लोकदृष्ट्यापि कर्मकृत् ।
jñānād galitakarmā yo lokadṛṣṭyāpi karmakṛt ,
नाप्नोत्यवसरं कर्त्रुं वक्तुमेव न किञ्चन ॥ १८-७७ ॥
nāpnotyavasaraṁ kartruṁ vaktumeva na kiñcana (18-77)

Although in the eyes of the world
the sage is seen to be performing duties,
in truth he serves no selfish purpose
when doing anything through body, speech, mind.
He has no aim to attain through any work done.
With the dawning of knowledge,
all karmas stand naturally dissolved for him.

क्व तमः क्व प्रकाशो वा हानं क्व च न किञ्चन ।
kva tamaḥ kva prakāśo vā hānaṁ kva ca na kiñcana ,
निर्विकारस्य धीरस्य निरातङ्कस्य सर्वदा ॥ १८-७८॥
nirvikārasya dhīrasya nirātaṅkasya sarvadā (18-78)

For the steadfast sage,
who abides fearless changeless steadfast within the Ātmā,
there exists nothing whatsoever except the Ātmā;
so for him then,
where is darkness?
...and where light?
...and where the reason to abdicate anything in sight?

क्व धैर्यं क्व विवेकित्वं क्व निरातङ्कतापि वा ।
kva dhairyaṁ kva vivekitvaṁ kva nirātaṅkatāpi vā ,
अनिर्वाच्यस्वभावस्य निःस्वभावस्य योगिनः ॥ १८-७९॥
anirvācyasvabhāvasya niḥsvabhāvasya yoginaḥ (18-79)

And where is patience, impatience?
and where discrimination, discernment, wisdom?
and where even fear and fearlessness
—unto the yogi whose real nature is that singular oneness
that is simply indescribable
...and who by his very characteristics is
without any characteristics?

न स्वर्गो नैव नरको जीवन्मुक्तिर्न चैव हि ।
na svargo naiva narako jīvanmuktirna caiva hi ,
बहुनात्र किमुक्तेन योगदृष्ट्या न किञ्चन ॥ १८-८०॥
bahunātra kimuktena yogadṛṣṭyā na kiñcana (18-80)

And where is heaven?
and where hell?
and where even this notion of *Jīvan-Mukti*—
liberation-while-still-alive?
Aye, there's nothing at all perceived of any consequence
in the consciousness of the yogi
who abides simply as the Ātmā pristine.
He simply is.

नैव प्रार्थयते लाभं नालाभेनानुशोचति ।
naiva prārthayate lābhaṁ nālābhenānuśocati ,
धीरस्य शीतलं चित्तममृतेनैव पूरितम् ॥ १८-८१ ॥
dhīrasya śītalaṁ cittamamṛtenaiva pūritam (18-81)

The sage seeks no gain,
nor does the lack of success cause him any pain;
verily that steady soul remains tranquil and reposed
—satiated in the fullness of the Ātmā-Rāma,
ever sustained by the nectar of Immortality
...of his own Self.

न शान्तं स्तौति निष्कामो न दुष्टमपि निन्दति ।
na śāntaṁ stauti niṣkāmo na duṣṭamapi nindati ,
समदुःखसुखस्तृप्तः किञ्चित् कृत्यं न पश्यति ॥ १८-८२ ॥
samaduḥkhasukhastṛptaḥ kiñcit kṛtyaṁ na paśyati (18-82)

The desireless person neither cozies up to the virtuous,
nor is he eager to damn the wicked and impious.
Remaining content and equanimous
in joys and in sorrows,
he finds nothing in the world
he must needs accomplish.
He simply abides blissful.

धीरो न द्वेष्टि संसारमात्मानं न दिदृक्षति ।
dhīro na dveṣṭi saṁsāramātmānaṁ na didṛkṣati ,
हर्षामर्षविनिर्मुक्तो न मृतो न च जीवति ॥ १८-८३ ॥
harṣāmarṣavinirmukto na mṛto na ca jīvati (18-83)

The steadfast sage doesn't abhor the world,
nor feels compelled to perceive the Self.
Free of joys, sorrows, ire, desire,
he is not in life—
and nor is he one who is counted among the dead.
He simply is.

निःस्नेहः पुत्रदारादौ निष्कामो विषयेषु च ।
nihsnehaḥ putradārādau niṣkāmo viṣayeṣu ca ,
निश्चिन्तः स्वशरीरेऽपि निराशः शोभते बुधः ॥ १८-८४ ॥
niścintaḥ svaśarīre'pi nirāśaḥ śobhate budhaḥ (18-84)

Not bound by any filial affections
nor by any objects of desires;
free from all expectations,
free even from the wants of body
—which the worldly people so fondly declare is 'mine'—
is the glorious all wise sage,
who is seen shining fiery in the resplendent
Fiery Light of Pure Consciousness.

तुष्टिः सर्वत्र धीरस्य यथापतितवर्तिनः ।
tuṣṭiḥ sarvatra dhīrasya yathāpatitavartinaḥ ,
स्वच्छन्दं चरतो देशान् यत्रस्तमितशायिनः ॥ १८-८५ ॥
svacchandaṁ carato deśān yatrastamitaśāyinaḥ (18-85)

Contented everywhere;
happy with whatever destiny brings his way—
the sage roams about at his leisure and pleasure;
and wherever the sun happens to set that day,
that is where he puts his head to rest.

पततूदेतु वा देहो नास्य चिन्ता महात्मनः ।
patatūdetu vā deho nāsya cintā mahātmanaḥ ,
स्वभावभूमिविश्रान्तिविस्मृताशेषसंसृतेः ॥ १८-८६ ॥
svabhāvabhūmiviśrāntivismṛtāśeṣasaṁsṛteḥ (18-86)

Reposing on the fundament of his own being,
reclining for the time being within the sheath of the body
—not quite caring if the body drops away from him,
or rises up with him again the next morning—
the great sage is oblivious of the rising-falling birth-death cycle,
abiding simply as the Ātmā, the Self.

अकिञ्चनः कामचारो निर्द्वन्द्वश्छिन्नसंशयः ।
akiñcanaḥ kāmacāro nirdvandvaśchinnasaṁśayaḥ ,
असक्तः सर्वभावेषु केवलो रमते बुधः ॥ १८-८७ ॥
asaktaḥ sarvabhāveṣu kevalo ramate budhaḥ (18-87)

Blessed is the all-wise sage
all whose doubts have been rent asunder,
who abides only in Onlyness,
attached to nothing,
without anything at all to call his own,
who moves about freely and at will,
ever free of the pair of opposites.

निर्ममः शोभते धीरः समलोष्टाश्मकाञ्चनः ।
nirmamaḥ śobhate dhīraḥ samaloṣṭāśmakāñcanaḥ ,
सुभिन्नहृदयग्रन्थिर्विनिर्धूतरजस्तमः ॥ १८-८८ ॥
subhinnahṛdayagranthirvinirdhūtarajastamaḥ (18-88)

Glory be to the steadfast sage,
devoid of the feelings of 'I' and 'mine';
to whom a clod of earth or gold or a stone,
are all of equal worth;
the knots of whose heart have been rent asunder,
and who has been purged of
the *rājasika* and the *tāmasika* elements.

सर्वत्रानवधानस्य न किञ्चिद् वासना हृदि ।
sarvatrānavadhānasya na kiñcid vāsanā hṛdi ,
मुक्तात्मनो वितृप्तस्य तुलना केन जायते ॥ १८-८९ ॥
muktātmano vitṛptasya tulanā kena jāyate (18-89)

Who can compare with that liberated sage who
—everywhere and at all times—
abides unconcerned and indifferent;
in whom abide no desires at all,
who remains totally detached and ever contented.

जानन्नपि न जानाति पश्यन्नपि न पश्यति ।
jānannapi na jānāti paśyannapi na paśyati ,
ब्रुवन्न् अपि न च ब्रूते कोऽन्यो निर्वासनादृते ॥ १८-९० ॥
bruvann api na ca brūte ko'nyo nirvāsanādṛte (18-90)

The sage of perfect understanding:
perceives—and yet he fathoms not;
he catches a sight—and yet he sees not;
and he utters words—and yet he talks not.
He ever abides bereft of desires and attachments
towards the things of the world.

भिक्षुर्वा भूपतिर्वापि यो निष्कामः स शोभते ।
bhikṣurvā bhūpatirvāpi yo niṣkāmaḥ sa śobhate ,
भावेषु गलिता यस्य शोभनाशोभना मतिः ॥ १८-९१ ॥
bhāveṣu galitā yasya śobhanāśobhanā matiḥ (18-91)

Whether he walks the earth as a mendicant or a king,
he alone shines glorious who remains unattached and
undesiring.
He from whom the occurrences of the world simply slither off
—without forming any impressions or judgments
as to what just happened was good or bad—
that wise one excels.

क्व स्वाच्छन्द्यं क्व सङ्कोचः क्व वा तत्त्वविनिश्चयः ।
kva svācchandyaṁ kva saṅkocaḥ kva vā tattvaviniścayaḥ ,
निर्व्याजार्जवभूतस्य चरितार्थस्य योगिनः ॥ १८-९२ ॥
nirvyājārjavabhūtasya caritārthasya yoginaḥ (18-92)

Where the ideas
of restraint,
or unbridled impunity,
or gaining wisdom
—for the yogi who has fulfilled the objective of human
existence?

...who has achieved the supreme end
...who has become
the embodiment of innocent virtuousness
—by becoming one in Brahama-Rāma.

आत्मविश्रान्तितृप्तेन निराशेन गतार्तिना ।
ātmaviśrāntitṛptena nirāśena gatārtinā ,
अन्तर्यदनुभूयेत तत् कथं कस्य कथ्यते ॥ १८-९३॥
antaryadanubhūyeta tat kathaṁ kasya kathyate (18-93)

In what way—and to whom—can be described
the inner state of the desireless sage
—whose sorrows have come to an end,
who abides fully content in the tranquility of the Ātmā?

सुप्तोऽपि न सुषुप्तौ च स्वप्नेऽपि शयितो न च ।
supto'pi na suṣuptau ca svapne'pi śayito na ca ,
जागरेऽपि न जागर्ति धीरस्तृप्तः पदे पदे ॥ १८-९४॥
jāgare'pi na jāgarti dhīrastṛptaḥ pade pade (18-94)

Not asleep even though in apparent slumber
—ever awake in the consciousness of the Self;
not lying down even when dreaming,
just watching this dream universe roll by
—awakened only within the Ātmā-Rāma;
never alert to the universe even when the eyes are open
—such is the steady sage
who abides complacent and aloof to the world under every condition.

ज्ञः सचिन्तोऽपि निश्चिन्तः सेन्द्रियोऽपि निरिन्द्रियः ।
jñaḥ sacinto'pi niścintaḥ sendriyo'pi nirindriyaḥ ,
सुबुद्धिरपि निर्बुद्धिः साहङ्कारोऽनहङ्कृतिः ॥ १८-९५॥
subuddhirapi nirbuddhiḥ sāhaṅkāro'nahaṅkṛtiḥ (18-95)

The sage who knows himself to be the Ātmā
—is free of senses even though possessed of sense-organs
—is free of thought even though having a mind
—is free of the mind even though birthed with ego
—is free of the ego even though possessed of consciousness.

Aye,
merging all these superimpositions away,
that steadfast yogi has rendered his consciousness pristinely pure:
becoming just the Ātmā-Rāma.

न सुखी न च वा दुःखी न विरक्तो न सङ्गवान् ।
na sukhī na ca vā duḥkhī na virakto na saṅgavān ,
न मुमुक्षुर्न वा मुक्ता न किञ्चिन्न च किञ्चन ॥ १८-९६ ॥
na mumukṣurna vā muktā na kiñcinnna ca kiñcana (18-96)

That blessed sage is:
neither glad nor sad,
neither attached nor detached,
neither liberated nor desirous of liberation.
Aye, he is neither into this, nor into that;
he is neither this, nor that
—he is simply the singular consciousness.
Abiding in bliss, he simply is.

विक्षेपेऽपि न विक्षिप्तः समाधौ न समाधिमान् ।
vikṣepe'pi na vikṣiptaḥ samādhau na samādhimān ,
जाड्येऽपि न जडो धन्यः पाण्डित्येऽपि न पण्डितः ॥ १८-९७ ॥
jāḍye'pi na jaḍo dhanyaḥ pāṇḍitye'pi na paṇḍitaḥ (18-97)

That blessed sage is:
—undistracted even amidst distractions
—unlost even when lost in deep meditations
—alive even though staying unmoving
—unlearned even though possessed of
the highest wisdom.

मुक्तो यथास्थितिस्वस्थः कृतकर्तव्यनिर्वृतः ।
mukto yathāsthitisvasthaḥ kṛtakartavyanirvṛtaḥ ,
समः सर्वत्र वैतृष्ण्यान्न स्मरत्यकृतं कृतम् ॥ १८-९८ ॥
samaḥ sarvatra vaitṛṣṇyānna smaratyakṛtaṁ kṛtam (18-98)

Adjudications
—such as what got done or not ...or what became undone—
do not even present themselves for consideration before the liberated Self-Realized yogi
who
—having embraced non-duality—
has gone beyond notions such as duties, actions, desires;
who under all conditions remains peaceful
—abiding only as the Ātmā-Rāma.

न प्रीयते वन्द्यमानो निन्द्यमानो न कुप्यति ।
na prīyate vandyamāno nindyamāno na kupyati ,
नैवोद्विजति मरणे जीवने नाभिनन्दति ॥१८-९९॥
naivodvijati maraṇe jīvane nābhinandati (18-99)

When praised, he feels no elation;
when blamed, he does not feel aggrieved or agitated;
that wise sage of steady wisdom
neither celebrates the enthrallments of life
nor fears the cold touch of death.

न धावति जनाकीर्णं नारण्यमुपशान्तधीः ।
na dhāvati janākīrṇaṁ nāraṇyamupaśāntadhīḥ ,
यथातथा यत्रतत्र सम एवावतिष्ठते ॥१८-१००॥
yathātathā yatratatra sama evāvatiṣṭhate (18-100)

The enlightened sage
neither seeks places filled with crowds,
nor hurries to forests or reprieves of the quiet.
At all times,
under all conditions,
in all places,
he in everyway remains in bliss:
unaffected unruffled quiet.

:: End Canto – XVIII ::

:: Canto – XIX ::
- Reposing as the Ātmā -

जनक उवाच
janaka uvāca:

तत्त्वविज्ञानसन्दंशमादाय हृदयोदरात् ।
tattvavijñānasandaṁśamādāya hṛdayodarāt ,
नाविधपरामर्शशल्योद्धारः कृतो मया ॥ १९-१ ॥
nāvidhaparāmarśaśalyoddhāraḥ kṛto mayā (19-1)

Janaka said:
Using the Pincer of Discernment
—right knowledge, pivoted to the Reality of Non-duality—
I have managed to extract and discard
—from in the inmost recesses of my heart—
the piercing thorns in the shape of dualities and divergent opinions
—thorns which otherwise distract one with their knifelike lacerations.

क्व धर्मः क्व च वा कामः क्व चार्थः क्व विवेकिता ।
kva dharmaḥ kva ca vā kāmaḥ kva cārthaḥ kva vivekitā ,
क्व द्वैतं क्व च वाऽद्वैतं स्वमहिम्नि स्थितस्य मे ॥ १९-२ ॥
kva dvaitaṁ kva ca vā'dvaitaṁ svamahimni sthitasya me (19-2)

Abiding only as the Ātmā-Rāma
—in my own fiery glory—
I perceive neither *Dharma*, nor *Kāma*,
nor *Artha* or *Viveka*.
And what of duality and non-duality?
I perceive nothing at all
save and except
the One Homogenized Existence,
One Complete Totality
—the Param-Ātmā-Rāma.

क्व भूतं क्व भविष्यद् वा वर्तमानमपि क्व वा ।
kva bhūtaṁ kva bhaviṣyad vā vartamānamapi kva vā ,
क्व देशः क्व च वा नित्यं स्वमहिम्नि स्थितस्य मे ॥ १९-३ ॥
kva deśaḥ kva ca vā nityaṁ svamahimni sthitasya me (19-3)

Where has the past vanished?
...and what of future?
...and where even has the present disappeared?
...and where is space?
...and what about time?
...and what even is eternity to me
—who am the Ātmā-Rāma,
abiding resplendent in my eternal essence?

क्व चात्मा क्व च वानात्मा क्व शुभं क्वाशुभं यथा ।
kva cātmā kva ca vānātmā kva śubhaṁ kvāśubhaṁ yathā ,
क्व चिन्ता क्व च वाचिन्ता स्वमहिम्नि स्थितस्य मे ॥ १९-४ ॥
kva cintā kva ca vācintā svamahimni sthitasya me (19-4)

Abiding only in the Bliss of Oneness in the Ātmā,
I have no consciousness either of the self
or of the non-self;
I know not what is auspicious and what inauspicious;
and I know not of anxiety or its opposite
or of any thought,
...or suffer from any lack thereof.

क्व स्वप्नः क्व सुषुप्तिर्वा क्व च जागरणं तथा ।
kva svapnaḥ kva suṣuptirvā kva ca jāgaraṇaṁ tathā ,
क्व तुरीयं भयं वापि स्वमहिम्नि स्थितस्य मे ॥ १९-५ ॥
kva turīyaṁ bhayaṁ vāpi svamahimni sthitasya me (19-5)

What and where the states of dream and deep sleep?
...and whither is the first state: wakefulness?
...and whither the fourth one: *Turiyā*?
...and where even is the dread of unknown for me?
—who only abide in my glorious essence
as The-One.

क्व दूरं क्व समीपं वा बाह्यं काभ्यन्तरं क्व वा ।
kva dūraṁ kva samīpaṁ vā bāhyaṁ kvābhyantaraṁ kva vā ,
क्व स्थूलं क्व च वा सूक्ष्मं स्वमहिम्नि स्थितस्य मे ॥ १९-६ ॥
kva sthūlaṁ kva ca vā sūkṣmaṁ svamahimni sthitasya me (19-6)

Where have proximity and distance disappeared?
...what is far? and what near?
...what and where is exterior and interior?
...what is gross and what subtle?
...they have all lost meaning for me
—who abide in my essence
as the Ātmā,
the fiery self-existent ever-abiding One-Consciousness.

क्व मृत्युर्जीवितं वा क्व लोकाः कास्य क्व लौकिकम् ।
kva mṛtyurjīvitaṁ vā kva lokāḥ kvāsya kva laukikam ,
क्व लयः क्व समाधिर्वा स्वमहिम्नि स्थितस्य मे ॥ १९-७ ॥
kva layaḥ kva samādhirvā svamahimni sthitasya me (19-7)

Where is life? and where death?
...and where relativity or the worldly phenomena?
...and where is meditation and the ensuant dissolution?
—for me, who am the Ātmā,
who ever abide resplendent in my glorious essence
as the Fiery Ocean of Consciousness.

अलं त्रिवर्गकथया योगस्य कथयाप्यलम् ।
alaṁ trivargakathayā yogasya kathayāpyalam ,
अलं विज्ञानकथया विश्रान्तस्य ममात्मनि ॥ १९-८ ॥
alaṁ vijñānakathayā viśrāntasya mamātmani (19-8)

Where's Dharma, Artha, Kāma?
...what need have I to bother with the three endeavors of human existence?
...or for gaining wisdom or a mastery in yoga?
—because I am already the Ātmā
—the self-sufficient all-pervading
resplendent Ocean of Existence.

:: End Canto – XIX ::

:: Canto – XX ::
- Liberation-in-Life -

जनक उवाच
janaka uvāca:

क्व भूतानि क्व देहो वा क्वेन्द्रियाणि क्व वा मनः ।
kva bhūtāni kva deho vā kvendriyāṇi kva vā manaḥ ,
क्व शून्यं क्व च नैराश्यं मत्स्वरूपे निरञ्जने ॥२०-१॥
kva śūnyaṁ kva ca nairāśyaṁ matsvarūpe nirañjane (20-1)

Janaka said:
Whither have disappeared the elements?
...to which place went the body?
...whither my senses?
and whither my mind?
...and whither is something, or anything at all?
... and whither any nihility and despondency?
—it has all vanished for me:
who am the Ātmā of untarnished glory,
the perfect being .

क्व शास्त्रं क्वात्मविज्ञानं क्व वा निर्विषयं मनः ।
kva śāstraṁ kvātmavijñānaṁ kva vā nirviṣayaṁ manaḥ ,
क्व तृप्तिः क्व वितृष्णात्वं गतद्वन्द्वस्य मे सदा ॥२०-२॥
kva tṛptiḥ kva vitṛṣṇātvaṁ gatadvandvasya me sadā (20-2)

Whither disappeared all the scriptures which led me here?
...whither the science of Self that emancipated me?
...where's the mind unattached to objects?
...and where even went the desirelessness and contentment
that delivered me to this realm?
Aye,
even the *sāttvika* goodness is all vanishing for me now
—because I fail to sense any duality at all
...anywhere in existence.

क्व विद्या क्व च वाविद्या क्वाहं क्वेदं मम क्व वा ।
kva vidyā kva ca vāvidyā kvāhaṁ kvedaṁ mama kva vā ,
क्व बन्ध क्व च वा मोक्षः स्वरूपस्य क्व रूपिता ॥२०-३॥
kva bandha kva ca vā mokṣaḥ svarūpasya kva rūpitā (20-3)

Whither went knowledge?
...and whither ignorance?
...and whither 'I' and 'this' and 'that'?
...and whither bondage?
...and whither liberation?
...and where the true form of me ...the correct definition of the self that I had all along been searching?
It's all fading, fading, fading ...

क्व प्रारब्धानि कर्माणि जीवन्मुक्तिरपि क्व वा ।
kva prārabdhāni karmāṇi jīvanmuktirapi kva vā ,
क्व तद् विदेहकैवल्यं निर्विशेषस्य सर्वदा ॥२०-४॥
kva tad videhakaivalyaṁ nirviśeṣasya sarvadā (20-4)

Whither has gone *prārabdha* karma—causality?
...whither the liberation-in-life?
...and whither even liberation after death?
None of it is there anymore for me:
who abide purely as the Totality of Brahama-Rāma,
totally undifferentiated.

क्व कर्ता क्व च वा भोक्ता निष्क्रियं स्फुरणं क्व वा ।
kva kartā kva ca vā bhoktā niṣkriyaṁ sphuraṇaṁ kva vā ,
क्वापरोक्षं फलं वा क्व निःस्वभावस्य मे सदा ॥२०-५॥
kvāparokṣaṁ phalaṁ vā kva niḥsvabhāvasya me sadā (20-5)

To which place went 'I' the doer?
...and whither is the enjoyer?
...and whither has disappeared activity,
...and whither the rise and ebb of thought?
...and whither is knowledge—direct or reflected?
—for me who am the Ātmā, bereft of ego.

क्व लोकं क्व मुमुक्षुर्वा क्व योगी ज्ञानवान् क्व वा ।
kva lokaṁ kva mumukṣurvā kva yogī jñānavān kva vā ,
क्व बद्धः क्व च वा मुक्तः स्वस्वरूपेऽहमद्वये ॥२०-६॥
kva baddhaḥ kva ca vā muktaḥ svasvarūpe'hamadvaye (20-6)

Whither went the world?
...and whither the aspirer who had been struggling for freedom?
...whither the contemplating yogi that used to be me?
...and whither the seer instilled with knowledge?
Where the Jīva suffering in bondages?
...and where the liberated soul?
—it's all the same to me now:
established in my innate immaculate Fiery Glory.

क्व सृष्टिः क्व च संहारः क्व साध्यं क्व च साधनम् ।
kva sṛṣṭiḥ kva ca saṁhāraḥ kva sādhyaṁ kva ca sādhanam ,
क्व साधकः क्व सिद्धिर्वा स्वस्वरूपेऽहमद्वये ॥२०-७॥
kva sādhakaḥ kva siddhirvā svasvarūpe'hamadvaye (20-7)

Whither has the creation disappeared?
...where went its remnants?
...where the destruction back to source?
...whatever happened to the goals of life?
...and where went the means to achieve them?
...and whither that aspirer full of purposes?
...and to which place vanished the achiever?
For me nothing has significance anymore—
now that I abide only as the Ātmā pure,
the One without a second.

क्व प्रमाता प्रमाणं वा क्व प्रमेयं क्व च प्रमा ।
kva pramātā pramāṇaṁ vā kva prameyaṁ kva ca pramā ,
क्व किञ्चित् क्व न किञ्चिद् वा सर्वदा विमलस्य मे ॥२०-८॥
kva kiñcit kva na kiñcid vā sarvadā vimalasya me (20-8)

Where is the knower?
...and where the object known?
...and where the means to its knowledge?
...and where the knowledge itself?
Where has it all vanished?
What is being and non-being for me
—who am the Ātmā of eternal perfection,
from whom all such considerations
have just simply melted away...

क्व विक्षेपः क्व चैकाग्र्यं क्व निर्बोधः क्व मूढता ।
kva vikṣepaḥ kva caikāgryaṁ kva nirbodhaḥ kva mūḍhatā ,
क्व हर्षः क्व विषादो वा सर्वदा निष्क्रियस्य मे ॥२०-९॥
kva harṣaḥ kva viṣādo vā sarvadā niṣkriyasya me (20-9)

Whither went concentration?
...and what happened to all those vexing distractions?
...whither the deluded soul?
...and whither the burdensome bag of delusions?
...where went the distracting charms and delights of the world?
...and where went sorrows?
For me, it has all coalesced into a Oneness.
Bereft of any karmas,
I am just the Ātmā now.

क्व चैष व्यवहारो वा क्व च सा परमार्थता ।
kva caiṣa vyavahāro vā kva ca sā paramārthatā ,
क्व सुखं क्व च वा दुखं निर्विमर्शस्य मे सदा ॥२०-१०॥
kva sukhaṁ kva ca vā dukhaṁ nirvimarśasya me sadā (20-10)

Whither the unrelenting stream of worldly affairs?
...and whither the transcendency from all that?
...and where are the revelries and miseries of life?
—for me, who am the Ātmā
beyond all deliberations and thoughts.

क्व माया क्व च संसारः क्व प्रीतिर्विरतिः क्व वा ।
kva māyā kva ca saṁsāraḥ kva prītirviratiḥ kva vā ,
क्व जीवः क्व च तद्ब्रह्म सर्वदा विमलस्य मे ॥२०-११॥
kva jīvaḥ kva ca tadbrahma sarvadā vimalasya me (20-11)

Whither went māyā?
...and whither went the world?
...and whither the entrapments and worldly attachments and detachments?
...and where even the notion of Jīva and Brahama?
—for me who abide now only as the Ātmā
perfect, pristine, pure.

क्व प्रवृत्तिर्निर्वृत्तिर्वा क्व मुक्तिः क्व च बन्धनम् ।
kva pravṛttirnirvṛttirvā kva muktiḥ kva ca bandhanam ,
कूटस्थनिर्विभागस्य स्वस्थस्य मम सर्वदा ॥२०-१२॥
kūṭasthanirvibhāgasya svasthasya mama sarvadā (20-12)

Whither dropped away activity & inactivity?
and attachments & struggles & renunciation?
And what of bondages & liberation?
It has all disappeared for me
—who abide simply rooted in my essence:
as the immutable indivisible Ātmā supreme.

कोपदेशः क्व वा शास्त्रं क्व शिष्यः क्व च वा गुरुः ।
kvopadeśaḥ kva vā śāstraṁ kva śiṣyaḥ kva ca vā guruḥ ,
क्व चास्ति पुरुषार्थो वा निरुपाधेः शिवस्य मे ॥२०-१३॥
kva cāsti puruṣārtho vā nirupādheḥ śivasya me (20-13)

Whither went instructions and the scriptural injunctions?
...whither disappeared the guru and disciple?
And what indeed is any object of life for me—
who am Shiva,
the inexpressible eternal Being
of supreme goodness.

— ❀ —

क्व चास्ति क्व च वा नास्ति क्वास्ति चैकं क्व च द्वयम् ।
kva cāsti kva ca vā nāsti kvāsti caikaṁ kva ca dvayam ,
बहुनात्र किमुक्तेन किञ्चिन्नोत्तिष्ठते मम ॥२०-१४॥
bahunātra kimuktena kiñcinnottiṣṭhate mama (20-14)

— ❀ —

Where is that which exists?
...and where is that which's non-existent?
Where is duality?
...and where non-duality—the One without a second, bereft of another?
Everything has gone, dropped, disappeared...
What more is there to say?
I am just the Ātmā,
and there is nothing at all tangible which emanates from that Ātmā...

Aye, in the end
...with the mind melded
...with thoughts, words, meanings all dissolved
only true quietude reigns.
When even the final fortification of the ego has fallen down
...with the 'I' submersed
...then everything fades away into arrant silence and blissfulness...
—and then the sage abides simply as the Param-Ātmā:
That Soundless Serene Ocean
of Existence-Bliss-Consciousness.

:: End Canto – XX ::

॥ इति श्रीअष्टावक्रविरचितं श्रीमदष्टावक्रगीता ॥

iti
śrīaṣṭāvakraviracitaṁ
śrīmadaṣṭāvakra gītā

Composed by

Ashtāvakra

this was the text of

Ashtāvakra Gītā

-: ॐ तत्सत् :-

-: aum tat-sat :-

ॐ AUM, That One [Alone Is] Real

www.ingramcontent.com/pod-product-compliance
Lightning Source LLC
Chambersburg PA
CBHW030334100526
44592CB00010B/697
* 9 7 8 1 9 4 5 7 3 9 4 8 4 *